CHANGES:
A Woman's Journal for Self-awareness and Personal Planning

Written by Mindy Bingham, Sandy Stryker
and Judy Edmondson
Edited by Barbara Greene, Kathleen Peters
and Kathy Araujo
Illustrated by Itoko Maeno, Janice Blair,
Diana Lackner and Pam Hoeft

Advocacy Press, Santa Barbara, California

For Charlotte, Amy, Jeri, Perri
and The One Hundred Committee

Copies of this book may be ordered by sending $14.45 ppd. to Changes, Advocacy Press, P.O. Box 236, Santa Barbara, CA 93102. (California residents add sales tax.)

Proceeds from the sale of this book will benefit the Girls Club of Santa Barbara, Inc. and contribute to the further development of programs for girls and young women aged 6 to 18.

 Published by Advocacy Press, P.O. Box 236, Santa Barbara, California 93102

Printed in the United States of America

12 11 10 9 8 7 6 5 4 3 2 1

GIRLS CLUBS OF AMERICA INC

This book belongs to _____

I began my entries on _____

I finished my entries on _____

This book is dedicated to _____

_____

_____

Changes is a revised version of our best-selling book *Choices: A Teen Woman's Journal for Self-awareness and Personal Planning.* (150,000 copies sold to date)

New Day

Within dawn's kaleidoscopic art
All universe becomes a part
Of an unfolding master plan
Begun the day that time began.
The ever changing harmony
Of dawn's celestial symphony
Tells me the secret I must know:

I too must change if I would grow
And learn the role that I must play
To bring the dawn to my new day.

William P. Sheehan

CONTENTS

"What I need is a change," said Barbara Ann Borden. She wasn't quite sure what kind of a change but, clearly, something had to be done. Once directed and purposeful, her life was now less satisfying than she knew it could be. She knew she could change. In the past few years, she'd seen her widowed mother take charge of her own life, one friend start a business, and another go back to school. But what should she do? Sometimes Barbara Ann felt she could take on the world. At other times she felt there was nothing she could do to make her life better.

Change is an interesting concept. It can make us feel at once excited and frightened, bold and vulnerable. We can embrace it or hide from it. But we cannot avoid it. Like everyone — like it or not — Barbara Ann had changed, was changing, and would continue to change throughout her life.

While no one can decide not to change, we can all, to a greater or lesser extent, decide how to change. What are the best changes for you to make now? This book is designed to help you decide — and then to help you make your changes successfully.

You may not have realized it yet, but this book is about you: your dreams, your thoughts, and your plans. To make it yours, you will need to be an active participant. We have included some exercises which have been helpful to other women. To make the most of your journey through this book, you should complete them as you read. There are also pages at the end of each section in which you are asked to record your own thoughts about the ideas just covered.

If you turn to the back of the book, you'll find pages that are not to be completed just now. They're there because, as long as you live, you will continue to grow and change. You'll have new opportunities, and new decisions to make. When the time comes, this section will help you make better decisions in your life.

We think you'll find this is a book you'll want to keep. Someday you may want to pass it on to your daughter or to another special young woman in your life. The final product will be the story of your life as planned, directed, and written by you. What could be more special than that?

I want to be all that I am capable
of becoming. . . .
— Katherine Mansfield
    Journal, 1922

INTRODUCTION

REFLECTIONS

CHAPTER ONE

Not Such Great Expectations

Attitudes and where they come from

It's hard to be a team player when they don't want you on their team.
— Rosabeth Moss Kanter

A long habit of not thinking a thing wrong gives it the superficial appearance of being right.
— Thomas Paine
Common Sense

As a little girl, did you ever wonder what became of Snow White, Cinderella, and Sleeping Beauty after they married their princes and retired to their respective castles? It's possible that they spent the rest of their lives happily playing bridge, experimenting with make-up, and redecorating the throne room. Yet, maybe one of them was forced to support the family when an unexpected revolution in the kingdom left her prince jobless. (Former princes are highly unemployable.) Maybe one of them was banished for being so fond of the castle pastry that she outgrew her royal cape. Or, perhaps, one grew so bored with the castle routine that she decided she needed to do something for herself.

If these things happened — and they might — what kind of jobs could they get? Like most women, they were brought up to believe that if they were cute and charming, someday their prince would appear. He would take care of them, provide for them, and worry about the future. In return, they gave up their independence and the ability to support themselves.

Today we know that being unable to support yourself is a risky way to live. Here's the bad news: As you know, about half of all marriages end in divorce. More married women now must work just to help pay the bills. Women outlive men by an average of about eight years. Of course, many women are choosing to skip marriage altogether in order to devote more time to their careers or other activities; but that's not necessarily bad news. The point, simply put, is that women need to be able to make enough money to support themselves.

Here's the good news: There are thousands of ways for you to do that. Today's women have more options for earning a livelihood than past generations. While only a few years ago most women who worked outside the home were found in only a few job categories — teaching, nursing, clerical work, or retail sales — it is now acceptable for a woman to be anything from an astronaut to a zoo keeper. Your imagination and ambition are the only limitations.

Look around you. Many women are combining careers with marriage and children. Others have decided not to marry at all. There are single-parent families, childless marriages, and families in which the woman has an outside job, while the man takes major responsibility for child care and housework. Which choices appeal to you most?

This book is devoted to helping you make the best decisions for *you*. The time for reshaping your future is *now*.

Your Life — Present and Future Visions

hat is your life like right now? How do you expect it to change in the years to come? The following exercise asks you to consider three important parts of your life — your living conditions, your primary activity, and the most significant people in your life — now and in the future.

Your living conditions refer to both your town and the kind of housing you have or want (apartment, home of your own, etc.). Would you like to live in another part of the country? Do you want to purchase a home sometime in the future?

Your primary activity refers to the way you spend most of your day, whether you are a full-time homemaker, hold a job outside the home, or balance career and family life. In a moment you're going to look ahead to view yourself in the future. When you do, be as specific as possible about what you might be doing. Could it be: Taking care of small children? Going back to school? Working as an accountant? Moving across the country? What would you find most rewarding?

The people closest to you need not be named. They might include spouse, parents, children, grandchildren or friends.

A chart for Cinderella showing her living conditions, activities and close relationships at various ages might look something like what you see here. After you read hers, try making one of your own.

CINDERELLA'S LIFE

Age	Where She Lives	Jobs or Major Activities	People Closest to Her
15	Humble cottage with many fireplaces	Taking orders Cleaning fireplaces Manicuring fingernails	Stepmother Stepsisters
20	Same as above	Growing pumpkins Raising white mice Taking charm course by correspondence Learning to walk in glass slippers without screaming in pain	Fairy Godmother
30	Castle	Raising young prince Trying to remain the way she was when the prince fell in love with her Soaking feet	Husband Son Therapist
40	Kingdom University	Taking art and design courses Starting consciousness-raising group Spending weekends with son	Son Friends
60	Co-op apt. in big city	Designing attractive and comfortable shoes for women Spending time with granddaughter, who will be the first princess to rule the kingdom	Friends Son Daughter-in-law Granddaughter

Now, make up a chart for yourself.

ENVISION YOUR LIFE

Age	Where You Live	Jobs or Major Activities	People Closest to You
Present			
3 years from now			
5 years from now			
10 years from now			
20 years from now			

You've just speculated about your future. Let's explore a little more. Keep your mind open. The sky's the limit!

Attitudes: Will Yours Limit Your Opportunities or Insure Your Success?

Your life choices are affected by attitudes — your own, and the world's. Because these attitudes play such an important part in your life, we must examine them carefully. Women today, as we have already noted, have more freedom and choices than ever before. Sometimes it can be confusing.

Since the changing role of women will affect your future, it's important to know how you feel now. Your opinions will create your attitude toward womanhood and work. Ultimately they will determine how you fit into the picture. To help sort out your opinions, complete the following exercise.

ATTITUDE INVENTORY[1]

Instructions: Put a check mark in the column that best describes how you feel.

	Strongly Agree	Agree	Undecided	Disagree	Strongly Disagree
1. Women with preschool children should not work outside the home.					
2. The mother should be awarded custody of the children when a couple is divorced.					
3. Divorced men should not have to assume support for their children.					
4. Men are more intelligent than women.					
5. If a working couple buys a house, the husband should make the house payments.					
6. At work, women are entitled to use sick leave for maternity leave.					
7. If a woman works outside the home, she should be responsible for the housework as well.					

	Strongly Agree	Agree	Undecided	Disagree	Strongly Disagree
8. I would vote for a woman for president if she were the best candidate.					
9. Women are less responsible than men.					
10. It is important for a man to be ``masculine'' and a woman to be ``feminine.''					
11. Men should not cry.					
12. Money spent on athletics should be evenly divided between boys and girls.					
13. Both men and women can be good doctors.					
14. Wives should make less money at their jobs than their husbands.					
15. Boys should have more education than girls.					
16. Women should not hold jobs on the night shift.					
17. Men should not do clerical work because they lack the necessary hand dexterity.					
18. Women can be capable administrators.					
19. Women should concentrate on finding jobs in the fields of nursing, teaching, clerical and secretarial work since they already possess these skills.					
20. A wife and husband should take turns staying home with a sick child.					
21. A single man is not capable of taking care of an infant.					

As you look back over your answers, take a moment to think about why you feel the way you do. Talk to your friends about your thoughts. Then think about your answers again.

By constantly examining your feelings, you continue to grow and learn.

Attitudes and Opinions: Where Do They Come From?

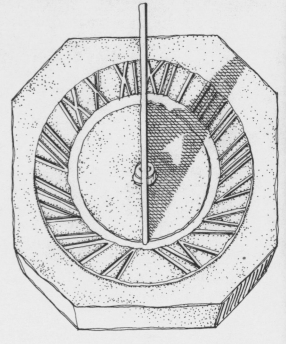

Your family, friends, society's expectations, your observations, TV, radio, newspapers and more, all have helped develop your opinions. We will examine some of these opinion-makers on the next pages.

Your Family

A four-year-old boy whose mother is a lawyer and whose father is a teacher announced, "I'm going to be a teacher when I grow up." "Why not a lawyer?" he was asked. "Only mommies are lawyers," he said.

When you were growing up, what you saw and heard within your own family greatly influenced *your* thoughts and feelings. Even if you disagreed with your family, you may have adopted many of its attitudes subconsciously.

What did you learn from your family? Do you want your own children to share these beliefs? The following exercise will help you decide.

Who is currently a member of your family (parents, spouse, children, step-children, grandchildren, etc.)?

_____

_____

If you don't have a family yet, whom would you include in your ideal family? For example, husband and two children? Husband but no children? Parents? Yourself only?

_____

_____

What messages or information did you receive from your family?

This may take a little detective work. Unless you were very lucky, your parents or other important adults in your life were unlikely to have sat down on the couch one Sunday afternoon and conducted a lecture on how they felt about life and what they wanted for you, complete with charts, graphs and handouts. If your parents had a happy marriage, however, you undoubtedly learned something from them. If your brother was encouraged to think about college, while you were encouraged to clean up your room or do something about your hair, you've learned something about sex roles, too. Was it more important to them that you made the honor roll, or that you had a date every Saturday night? Were there often arguments in your family? What were they usually about? What messages did your parents convey about the kind of work women should do? What did they tell you about your own potential? Think about the way everyone in your family treated everyone else. How did you feel about that treatment?

When you were growing up, what messages or information did you receive from your mother and other adult women about the importance of the following:

Success in school? _____
_____

Appearance? _____
_____

Marriage? _____
_____

Career? _____
_____

Children? _____
_____

When you were growing up, what messages or information did you receive from your father and other adult males about the importance of the following:

Success in school? _____
_____

Appearance? _____
_____

Marriage? _____
_____

Career? _____
_____

Children? _____
_____

What messages would you give your daughter or granddaughter about the importance of the following:

Success in school? _____

_____

_____

Appearance? _____

_____

_____

Marriage? _____

_____

_____

Career? _____

_____

_____

Children? _____

_____

_____

What about our Peers?

Our friends and colleagues have a strong influence on our attitudes. Interview two women who are important to you. One of the women you interview should currently have a full-time job. Discover how they felt about being women as they were growing up and how they feel about the roles of women today.

PERSON I INTERVIEWED: _____

RELATIONSHIP: _____

DATE: _____

ASK THESE QUESTIONS:

Do you think girls are raised differently than boys? If so, in what ways?

_____

_____

Do you think you were treated differently because you were a girl?

_____

_____

Should women prepare for a career outside the home? Why or why not?

_____

_____

If you could relive your life, what changes would you make in it?

_____

_____

Women play many important roles in their lives. Which do you think should be most important?

_____

_____

If you were going to give me one piece of advice about my future, what would it be?

_____

_____

PERSON I INTERVIEWED: _____

RELATIONSHIP: _____

DATE: _____

ASK THESE QUESTIONS:

Do you think girls are raised differently than boys? If so, in what ways?

_____

_____

Do you think you were treated differently because you were a girl?

_____

_____

Should women prepare for a career? Why or why not?

_____

_____

If you could relive your life, what changes would you make in it?

_____

_____

Women play many important roles in their lives. Which do you think should be most important?

_____

_____

If you were going to give me one piece of advice, what would it be?

_____

_____

Your attitudes are influenced by what you see around you, as well as by your family.

Have You Ever Met a Woman Truck Driver?

Our own observations give us much true and needed information. You may have observed, for instance, that tragedy can be avoided if you remove your make-up *before* taking off your expensive, new, white turtleneck sweater. But some of the ideas we acquire through observation are false. Because you rarely meet a woman truck driver or a male nurse, you may think that such people do not exist, or, if they do, that they are weird. That's natural. You grew up in a world in which it was "normal" for *men* to be truck drivers and *women* to be nurses. There comes a time when you must question what you see. If something is "normal," is it automatically right and proper? If it is not typical, is it necessarily wrong?

Although your feelings are not easily changed, it's important to consider why you feel as you do. By answering the following questions, you may gain some insight into your attitudes. You may even open your eyes to a whole new world of choices.

Is it right for *only* men to be truck drivers? What is there about the job that makes it unsuitable for a woman?

_____

_____

_____

Would you like to be a truck driver? Why or why not?

_____

_____

_____

Look back at what you just wrote. Were the reasons you gave based on what a truck driver actually does on the job?

_____

_____

_____

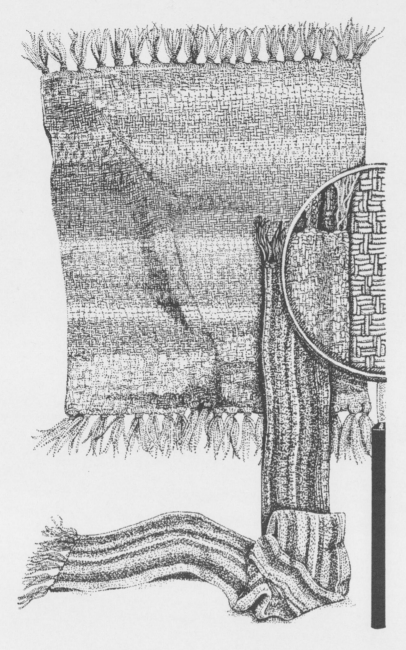

Did you know that the world is populated primarily by males, professionals, whites and members of the middle class? Did you know that women make up only 28 percent of the population; that one-half of all women are teenagers or in their early twenties; that more than one-third are unemployed or have no identifiable purpose beyond offering emotional support to men or serving as objects of sexual desire; that minorities are generally service workers, criminals, victims or students; that the elderly are usually infirm, senile, or helpless? If you watch much TV, these are the impressions you get daily on the "tube".[2]
— Dennis Coon
Introduction to Psychology: Exploration and Application

Every time you watch TV or open a magazine, you learn something about what it means to be a woman. What you learn is not necessarily *true*, you understand. As the paragraph above shows, the world portrayed by television bears little resemblance to the world in which we live. Women, for example, make up 51 percent of the population in our country. They come in all sizes, shapes, and ages. In fact, women live an average of seven years longer than men. Most women in the United States work outside the home.

Although you may not realize it, the imaginary world we see on TV makes a deep impression. If all women have glamorous jobs, exciting personal lives and perfect children, you are likely to believe that being a "superwoman" is the norm. You might feel like a failure if your own life bears little resemblance to this stereotype, or you might exhaust yourself trying to live up to an ideal that is unattainable. Next time you see your favorite heroine on TV, ask yourself, "How realistic is her lifestyle?"

Take a closer look at the images of men and women commonly created by the media. If you like, make a collage by pasting pictures and words from magazines and newspapers which show how men and women are typically portrayed. Don't forget to consider TV and movies as well as printed materials.

Once upon a time . . .

We have been receiving these messages all of our lives. As children, many of us heard the same stories over and over again. Those nursery rhymes and fairy tales affect our present beliefs more than you might think. The more often you hear something, the more likely you are to remember it. And, on a subconscious level, at least, you begin to believe it. After awhile, you will even start repeating the message to yourself. And the tapes that run in your mind will begin to affect your conscious actions.

Consider our old friend, the prince, for example. He trotted through many of the fairy tales we heard as children. If you were to ask women if they believe in him, they would almost certainly deny it. Their actions, however, might lead you to believe otherwise. Millions of women have not prepared themselves to be self-supporting, presumably because they expect someone else to come along (preferably in a fancy car rather than on a white charger) to take care of them.

The phrases below are examples of some of the messages related by many children's stories. Draw a line from the message or myth in the left column to the appropriate source in the right column. There may be more than one source for each message.

MESSAGES

Some day my prince will come.
And they lived happily ever after.
Women are vain and jealous.
Step-parents are evil.
Women belong in castles and towers.
Men belong on thrones or horses.
Women get what they want through magic or
    scheming or being "nice".
Men get what they want through work and bravery.
Women must have long hair and small feet.
Women can't get along with each other.
Men work well together.
Women are self-sacrificing.
Men go after what they want.
It's dangerous for girls to have adventures.

SOURCES

Cinderella

Snow White

Rapunzel

Sleeping Beauty

Hansel and Gretel

Beauty and the Beast

Little Red Riding Hood

Goldilocks and the Three Bears

Can you think of other messages? Other sources?

_____   _____

_____   _____

Reprinted with permission
© *More Choices: A Strategic Guide for Mixing Career and Family.*   Bingham and Stryker

What TV Tells You

Every time you watch TV you receive messages about which jobs are considered proper for women. Watch for two hours, then complete the following exercise. Repeat this activity several times during the next month, and see what pattern emerges.

SHOW	CHARACTER	SEX	ROLE OR OCCUPATION

COMMERCIAL	CHARACTER	SEX	ROLE OR OCCUPATION

What did you learn from this exercise?

What "Kid-Vid" (TV for Children) Tells You

If you had a TV set when you were a child, it too may have taught you how to think about proper roles for girls and boys. Children today are apt to receive similar messages. On Saturday morning, watch the kiddie shows and commercials. What do they tell you about differences between boys and girls? Record your observations below.

COMMERCIAL OR SHOW	CHARACTER	SEX	PRODUCT ADVERTISED OR CHARACTER'S ACTIVITY
_____	_____	_____	_____
_____	_____	_____	_____
_____	_____	_____	_____
_____	_____	_____	_____
_____	_____	_____	_____
_____	_____	_____	_____
_____	_____	_____	_____

What careers do commercials seem to encourage boys to pursue through their play?

_____

_____

What career options are shown for girls through play?

_____

_____

Have any of the advertisers shown girls playing with trucks, building materials or other "boy-oriented toys"?

Yes _____ No _____ If yes, which? _____

Have any of the advertisers shown boys playing with dolls, toy appliances or other "girl-oriented toys"?

Yes _____ No _____ If yes, which? _____

Textbooks and what you learned in school also influenced your opinions. Let's look at history, the study of events and people from the past.

When you read history books, did you ever wonder where all the *women* were? You'd almost think that, until just recently, the world was inhabited almost entirely by men (who apparently were dropped here from a passing space ship, or sprouted out of the ground, like carrots). When a woman made an appearance in history books, she usually stayed just long enough to be burned at the stake or have her head chopped off.

Women, of course, have always existed. They've worked hard and played an important role in the development of our world. Women have been queens and explorers, leaders in battle, artists and musicians, writers and scientists, spies and outlaws, teachers and athletes, and just about anything else you can name. That's important for you to remember. Women may have been neglected or repressed in history books, but that doesn't mean they haven't made history.

In the next exercise, see if you can fill in the names of both men and women who have become famous for their work in each of the categories listed. If it's easier to think of men than women (and most likely it will be), remember that is partly due to the emphasis history has given men's achievements.

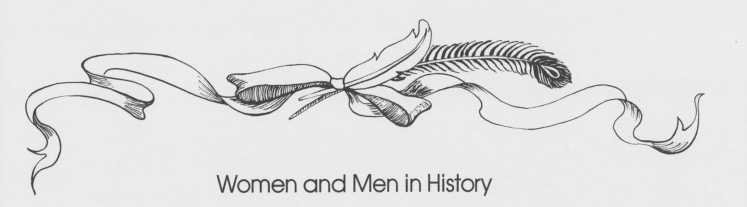

Women and Men in History

EXPLORERS:

Female _____ Male _____

MILITARY LEADERS:

Female _____ Male _____

MUSICAL COMPOSERS:

Female _____ Male _____

NATIONAL LEADERS (prior to 1850):

Female _____ Male _____

FAMOUS KINGS AND QUEENS (prior to 1850):

Female _____ Male _____

EARLY AMERICAN COLONIAL LEADERS:

Female _____ Male _____

CURRENT NATIONAL LEADERS:

Female _____ Male _____

INFAMOUS VILLAINS:

Female _____ Male _____

ATHLETES:

Female _____ Male _____

UNITED STATES SENATORS:

Female _____ Male _____

AUTHORS:

Female _____ Male _____

What Qualities Does a Woman Possess?

What are the characteristics of "normal" men and women? Let's examine your perceptions.

Are women typically emotional or unemotional? How about men? Do you think they are usually emotional? Or unemotional? The following exercise, based on a study called the *Broverman Scale*,[3] will help you visualize the differences you perceive between the sexes. In the left hand column is one list of characteristics. Their opposites are listed in the right hand column. On the lines between, put a check mark to indicate how you would rate a typical man on that scale. For example, if you think most men are aggressive, mark the space nearest that word. If you think they are non-aggressive, mark the space at the opposite end of the scale. If you think most men rank somewhere between, mark whatever place you think is appropriate. Then go on to the second set and repeat the exercise; this time show how you think a typical woman would rate.

BROVERMAN SHORT FORM CHARACTERISTIC SCALE

This scale has seven spaces between each pair of opposing characteristics. For each pair, mark one of the seven spaces, basing your choice on which space best describes "normal" or typical males. Use the middle space only if you feel the traits occur equally in men and women.

MALE

Aggressive	___ ___ ___ ___ ___ ___ ___	Non-aggressive
Independent	___ ___ ___ ___ ___ ___ ___	Dependent
Emotional	___ ___ ___ ___ ___ ___ ___	Unemotional
Subjective	___ ___ ___ ___ ___ ___ ___	Objective
Submissive	___ ___ ___ ___ ___ ___ ___	Dominant
Excitable	___ ___ ___ ___ ___ ___ ___	Non-excitable
Competitive	___ ___ ___ ___ ___ ___ ___	Non-competitive
Easily hurt	___ ___ ___ ___ ___ ___ ___	Not easily hurt
Adventurous	___ ___ ___ ___ ___ ___ ___	Cautious
Leader	___ ___ ___ ___ ___ ___ ___	Follower
Not appearance-oriented	___ ___ ___ ___ ___ ___ ___	Appearance-oriented

BROVERMAN SHORT FORM CHARACTERISTIC SCALE

This scale has seven spaces between each pair of opposing characteristics. For each pair, mark one of the seven spaces, basing your choice on which space best describes "normal" or typical females. Use the middle space only if you feel the traits occur equally in men and women.

FEMALE

Aggressive	___ ___ ___ ___ ___ ___ ___	Non-aggressive
Independent	___ ___ ___ ___ ___ ___ ___	Dependent
Emotional	___ ___ ___ ___ ___ ___ ___	Unemotional
Subjective	___ ___ ___ ___ ___ ___ ___	Objective
Submissive	___ ___ ___ ___ ___ ___ ___	Dominant
Excitable	___ ___ ___ ___ ___ ___ ___	Non-excitable
Competitive	___ ___ ___ ___ ___ ___ ___	Non-competitive
Easily hurt	___ ___ ___ ___ ___ ___ ___	Not easily hurt
Adventurous	___ ___ ___ ___ ___ ___ ___	Cautious
Leader	___ ___ ___ ___ ___ ___ ___	Follower
Not appearance-oriented	___ ___ ___ ___ ___ ___ ___	Appearance-oriented

How About a Healthy Adult?

Repeat the exercise again, this time rating a healthy adult. How would a well-adjusted, mature person rate on this scale?

BROVERMAN SHORT FORM CHARACTERISTIC SCALE

This scale has seven spaces between each pair of opposing characteristics. For each pair, mark one of the seven spaces, basing your choice on which space best describes "normal" healthy adults. Use the middle space only if you feel the traits occur equally in men and women.

HEALTHY ADULT

Aggressive	_____ _____ _____ _____ _____ _____	Non-aggressive
Independent	_____ _____ _____ _____ _____ _____	Dependent
Emotional	_____ _____ _____ _____ _____ _____	Unemotional
Subjective	_____ _____ _____ _____ _____ _____	Objective
Submissive	_____ _____ _____ _____ _____ _____	Dominant
Excitable	_____ _____ _____ _____ _____ _____	Non-excitable
Competitive	_____ _____ _____ _____ _____ _____	Non-competitive
Easily hurt	_____ _____ _____ _____ _____ _____	Not easily hurt
Adventurous	_____ _____ _____ _____ _____ _____	Cautious
Leader	_____ _____ _____ _____ _____ _____	Follower
Not appearance-oriented	_____ _____ _____ _____ _____ _____	Appearance-oriented

After reviewing your answers, what do you conclude about a healthy adult?

Inge and Donald Broverman and several co-workers gave 79 psychologists (46 male and 33 female) the rating scales you just completed.* The psychologists' ratings for "healthy, mature adult men" were very similar to those for "healthy adult with sex unspecified." The "healthy, mature adult woman," on the other hand, differed from both men and adults. The psychologists rated women as more submissive, more emotional, more easily influenced, more excitable in a minor crisis, more vain, more easily hurt emotionally, less objective, less independent, less adventurous, less competitive and less aggressive. To top things off, they said women exhibit a dislike of math and science.

These results show that the psychologists believed dependency, passivity and submissiveness are normal characteristics of healthy mature women, but not of their male counterparts, *nor* of adults in general. The Brovermans' study implies that sex-role stereotyping limits healthy functioning and development.

* The rating scales used here are abbreviated.

To compare your ratings with those of friends, assign the numerical values 1, 2, 3, 4, 5, 6, and 7 to each line (left to right).

Example:

Aggressive   1   2   3   4   5   6   7   Non-aggressive

Add the numbers you and your group checked for each of the characteristics listed. For example, if for "aggressive — non-aggressive" the six people in your group checked the spaces 2, 2, 3, 1, 2, 2, on the page labeled "male," the average rating would be 2. (2 + 2 + 3 + 1 + 2 + 2 = 12 and 12 divided by 6 = 2.) This would show that those taking the survey think males are fairly aggressive. (An average of 4 indicates a middle score, halfway between the two extremes.) Find the average for each characteristic listed on all three tests.

Now rate *yourself*. For each pair of characteristics, mark the space you feel best indicates your personality.

Your Name _____

Aggressive	___	___	___	___	___	___	Non-aggressive
Independent	___	___	___	___	___	___	Dependent
Emotional	___	___	___	___	___	___	Unemotional
Subjective	___	___	___	___	___	___	Objective
Submissive	___	___	___	___	___	___	Dominant
Excitable	___	___	___	___	___	___	Non-excitable
Competitive	___	___	___	___	___	___	Non-competitive
Easily hurt	___	___	___	___	___	___	Not easily hurt
Adventurous	___	___	___	___	___	___	Cautious
Leader	___	___	___	___	___	___	Follower
Not appearance-oriented	___	___	___	___	___	___	Appearance-oriented

Do *your* characteristics differ from those you attributed to a "Healthy Adult"? If so, maybe you should consider ways you can strengthen or change your characteristics to match your feelings about what is healthy.

How do your family and friends feel about men and women? We've included another copy of the exercise so you can make copies and conduct your own test. You can't help but be affected by the feelings of those closest to you. They naturally want you to be a mature and happy person. Yet without meaning to, they may be sending you — and themselves — the wrong kinds of messages about what is proper or appropriate behavior. If they are, they may be just as surprised to learn it as you were!

BROVERMAN SHORT FORM CHARACTERISTIC SCALE

This scale has seven spaces between each pair of opposing characteristics. For each pair, mark one of the seven spaces, basing your choice on which space best describes "normal" or typical males. Use the middle space only if you feel the traits occur equally in men and women.

MALE

Aggressive	_____ _____ _____ _____ _____ _____ _____	Non-aggressive
Independent	_____ _____ _____ _____ _____ _____ _____	Dependent
Emotional	_____ _____ _____ _____ _____ _____ _____	Unemotional
Subjective	_____ _____ _____ _____ _____ _____ _____	Objective
Submissive	_____ _____ _____ _____ _____ _____ _____	Dominant
Excitable	_____ _____ _____ _____ _____ _____ _____	Non-excitable
Competitive	_____ _____ _____ _____ _____ _____ _____	Non-competitive
Easily hurt	_____ _____ _____ _____ _____ _____ _____	Not easily hurt
Adventurous	_____ _____ _____ _____ _____ _____ _____	Cautious
Leader	_____ _____ _____ _____ _____ _____ _____	Follower
Not appearance-oriented	_____ _____ _____ _____ _____ _____ _____	Appearance-oriented

BROVERMAN SHORT FORM CHARACTERISTIC SCALE

This scale has seven spaces between each pair of opposing characteristics. For each pair, mark one of the seven spaces, basing your choice on which space best describes "normal" or typical females. Use the middle space only if you feel the traits occur equally in men and women.

FEMALE

Aggressive	_____ _____ _____ _____ _____ _____ _____	Non-aggressive
Independent	_____ _____ _____ _____ _____ _____ _____	Dependent
Emotional	_____ _____ _____ _____ _____ _____ _____	Unemotional
Subjective	_____ _____ _____ _____ _____ _____ _____	Objective
Submissive	_____ _____ _____ _____ _____ _____ _____	Dominant
Excitable	_____ _____ _____ _____ _____ _____ _____	Non-excitable
Competitive	_____ _____ _____ _____ _____ _____ _____	Non-competitive
Easily hurt	_____ _____ _____ _____ _____ _____ _____	Not easily hurt
Adventurous	_____ _____ _____ _____ _____ _____ _____	Cautious
Leader	_____ _____ _____ _____ _____ _____ _____	Follower
Not appearance-oriented	_____ _____ _____ _____ _____ _____ _____	Appearance-oriented

BROVERMAN SHORT FORM CHARACTERISTIC SCALE

This scale has seven spaces between each pair of opposing characteristics. For each pair, mark one of the seven spaces, basing your choice on which space best describes "normal" healthy adults. Use the middle space only if you feel completely neutral or evenly divided.

HEALTHY ADULT

Aggressive	___ ___ ___ ___ ___ ___ ___	Non-aggressive
Independent	___ ___ ___ ___ ___ ___ ___	Dependent
Emotional	___ ___ ___ ___ ___ ___ ___	Unemotional
Subjective	___ ___ ___ ___ ___ ___ ___	Objective
Submissive	___ ___ ___ ___ ___ ___ ___	Dominant
Excitable	___ ___ ___ ___ ___ ___ ___	Non-excitable
Competitive	___ ___ ___ ___ ___ ___ ___	Non-competitive
Easily hurt	___ ___ ___ ___ ___ ___ ___	Not easily hurt
Adventurous	___ ___ ___ ___ ___ ___ ___	Cautious
Leader	___ ___ ___ ___ ___ ___ ___	Follower
Not appearance oriented	___ ___ ___ ___ ___ ___ ___	Appearance oriented

REFLECTIONS

You'll find a page entitled "Reflections" at the end of each chapter.
Use it to jot down your thoughts and feelings about what you've just
learned. Or, use it for poetry, artwork, snapshots or whatever is
meaningful to you.

CHAPTER TWO

Being a Woman Isn't Always Easy

Greater awareness can help you handle choices

...Who wouldn't want a wife?
— Judy Syfers
  Writer

I don't ride to beat the boys,
just to win.
— Denise Boudrot
  Jockey

It's O.K. for Women to Want a Career

Betty Sue's Story

Betty Sue was extremely concerned about her femininity. She had thirteen sweaters in various shades of pink, batted her long, expertly-applied eyelashes constantly, and had perfected a giggle that made some people want to slug her right behind her delicately scented, sea shell-like little ears. Of course, no one ever did it because Betty Sue looked as if she would shatter like crystal at the slightest touch.

When she was eighteen, Betty Sue married a man who owned a construction company. Betty Sue's husband supplied her with buckets of perfume, closets full of satin negligees and high-heeled slippers, and every shade of nail polish Revlon produced. Then suddenly, her husband was killed in an airplane crash. At first Betty Sue didn't know what to do. She soon made a courageous decision. She would take over her husband's business. Everyone laughed, saying she'd change her mind as soon as she broke her first fingernail. Betty Sue surprised them all. She learned to operate heavy equipment, to read plans, to bid on jobs, to hire, fire, and negotiate with unions; and she made the company more successful than ever before.

How did Betty Sue feel about her "new self"? Whenever anyone asked if she felt badly about appearing unfeminine, she said, "This is what feminine looks like."

Somewhere along the road, the meaning of the word "feminine" has become confused. It doesn't mean weak or helpless or dumb. It simply means belonging to the female sex.

Since you are female, anything you do — or are capable of doing — may be considered "feminine." Of course the roles of wife and mother are traditionally feminine. Being a truck driver, mechanic, doctor, or physicist can be just as feminine, simply because women have already proved that they are capable of such work.

Just as you'll hear many misconceptions about what a woman *should be*, there are also many silly notions about what women *can do*. After all, what would we do if there were a national crisis and the president were getting her legs waxed at Elizabeth Arden's? Could a woman be an airline pilot? How silly. Everyone knows she'd burst into tears and give up if she ran into a thunderstorm over Indianapolis! Does this sound ridiculous? It *is* ridiculous. Just the same there are still people around who think that way. Don't *you* be one of them. Putting irrational limits on your aspirations will only make you feel less worthy as a person, and it will *cost you money*.

The Working World

"When I grow up, I want to be a _____." You can usually tell the sex of a person by the way he or she completes that sentence. Why? When you look at the working world today, most occupations are still dominated by one sex or the other. Below is a list of jobs. Read through it and put an F by jobs usually held by women, and an M by those jobs usually held by men. At this point in your journal we hope you are saying to yourself, "I don't see jobs as either male or female." For this exercise though, consider how the world is today.

What do you see when you walk into a hospital? You see doctors M. and nurses F. Likewise, most secretaries are women. Put an F by secretary. When you walk into a bank, what do you see? It's tellers F and bank officers M.

Keep in mind that, just because a pattern exists, there is no reason for you to assume that it is carved in stone. Changes are taking place in all fields.

_____	Architect	_____	Elementary school teacher
_____	Telephone installer	_____	Carpenter
_____	Engineer	_____	Painter (Construction)
_____	Clerk-typist	_____	Air traffic controller
_____	Bookkeeper	_____	Airplane mechanic
_____	Secretary	_____	Pilot
_____	Computer programmer	_____	Flight attendant
_____	Dental assistant	_____	Truck driver
_____	Bank teller	_____	Nurse
_____	Mail carrier	_____	Doctor
_____	Lawyer	_____	Receptionist

Now let's attach salaries to these jobs. The salaries given below are from the 1986-87 *Occupational Outlook Handbook* published by the U.S. Department of Labor. These figures represent the average salary based on 1984-1985 surveys.

Using the figures listed, complete a graph of salaries on the following page. Use a *pen* for each dot that represents a "woman's job" as identified by the symbol F. Use a *pencil* for each dot that represents a "man's job" as identified by the symbol M. Connect the pencil dots with pencil and the pen dots with pen. (Colored pens or pencils may be used instead of plain pens and pencils.)

AVERAGE ANNUAL SALARIES

Architect	$29,000
Telephone installer	$27,000
Engineer	$41,000
Typist	$15,000
Bookkeeper	$13,500
Secretary	$17,000
Computer Programmer	$26,000
Dental Assistant	$12,000
Bank Teller	$11,000
Lawyer	$88,000
Mail Carrier	$25,000
Elementary School Teacher	$23,000
Carpenter	$25,000
Painter (Construction)	$16,000
Air Traffic Controller	$35,000
Airplane Mechanic	$25,000
Pilot	$80,000
Flight Attendant	$23,000
Truck Driver (Long Distance)	$25,000
Nurse	$21,000
Doctor	$108,000
Receptionist	$14,000

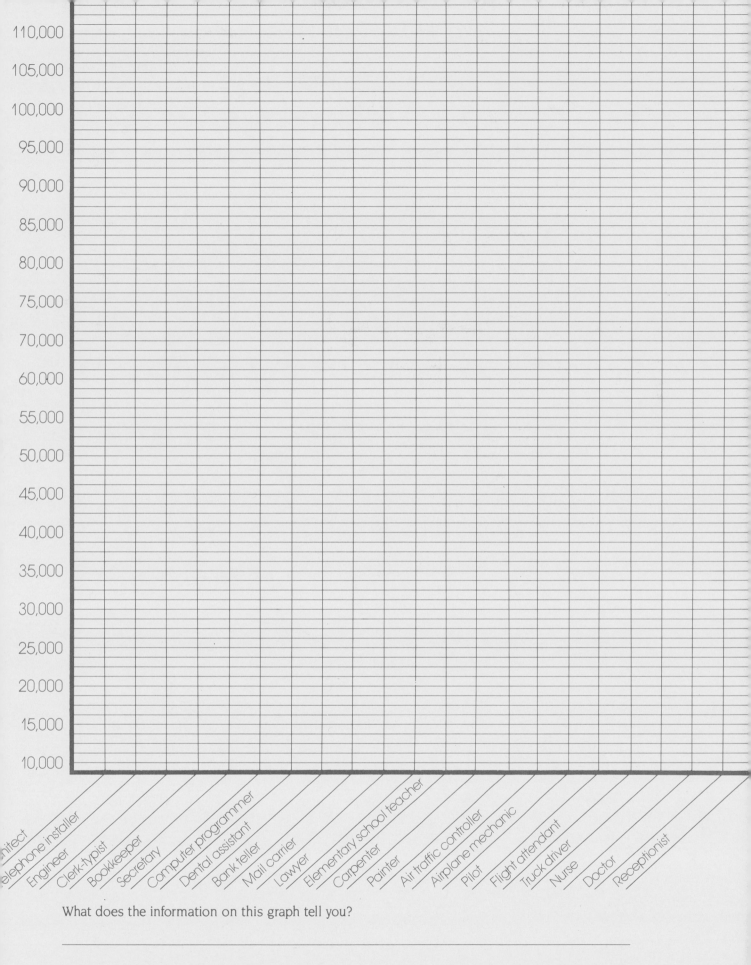

110,000	
105,000	
100,000	
95,000	
90,000	
85,000	
80,000	
75,000	
70,000	
60,000	
55,000	
50,000	
45,000	
40,000	
35,000	
30,000	
25,000	
20,000	
15,000	
10,000	

Architect · Telephone installer · Engineer · Clerk-typist · Bookkeeper · Secretary · Computer programmer · Dental assistant · Bank teller · Mail carrier · Lawyer · Elementary school teacher · Carpenter · Painter · Air traffic controller · Airplane mechanic · Pilot · Flight attendant · Truck driver · Nurse · Doctor · Receptionist

What does the information on this graph tell you?

_____

_____

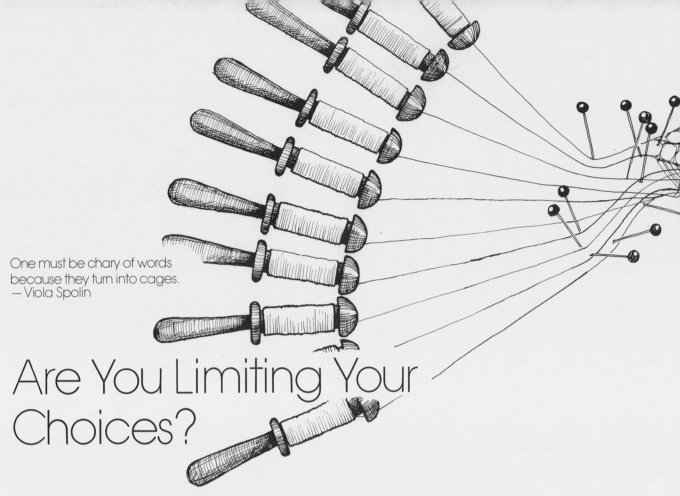

One must be chary of words
because they turn into cages.
— Viola Spolin

Are You Limiting Your Choices?

If you're good with numbers, why shouldn't you consider being an accountant instead of a bookkeeper? If you're interested in medicine, why immediately presume that you have to be a nurse? This is the time for you to explore and to dream. What would you want to be if you were a man? As a woman is there any *real* reason why you shouldn't be the same thing? Why should your sex stand in the way of becoming anything you want to be?

COMMENTS:

_____

_____

_____

_____

_____

_____

_____

_____

_____

_____

_____

_____

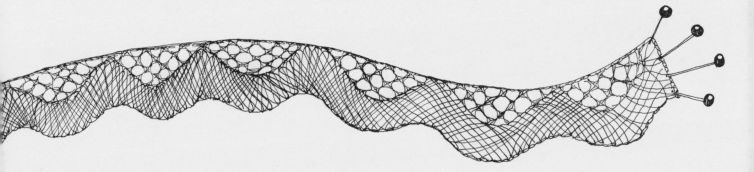

How much do you know about working women today? Take this quiz to find out.

WOMEN IN THE WORKFORCE

1. The number of women who work for pay at some time during their lives is
   a. 3 out of 10
   b. 5 out of 10
   c. 7 out of 10
   d. 9 out of 10

2. In 1985 the percentage of women who worked because of economic need (self-supporting or husband earned less than $15,000) was
   a. 33 percent
   b. 45 percent
   c. 56 percent
   d. 67 percent

3. Married men with non-working wives and one or more children make up what percentage of all households?
   a. 9.9 percent
   b. 26.4 percent
   c. 62.8 percent
   d. 79.3 percent

4. Women make up what percentage of the total workforce?
   a. 15 percent
   b. 24 percent
   c. 44 percent
   d. 50 percent

5. In 1984, the median earnings for men and women who worked full-time, year-round were
   a. men — $26,456,   women — $24,954
   b. men — $23,218,   women — $14,780
   c. men — $22,317,   women — $19,942
   d. men — $20,561,   women — $20,240

6. In the past decade, three-fifths of the labor force increase has been among
   a. women
   b. minority women
   c. minorities
   d. married women

7. In 1985, fully employed, female high school graduates (with no college background) earned
   a. more than male high school graduates
   b. less than men who did not complete elementary school
   c. more than male high shool graduates, but less than male college graduates
   d. about the same as male high school graduates

8. The absentee rate from work for women is
   a. much greater than for men
   b. slightly more than for men
   c. much less than for men
   d. slightly less than for men

9. The unemployment rate of minority women, compared to that of Caucasian women, is
   a. about the same
   b. less than the rate for Caucasian women
   c. 35 percent more
   d. twice as high

10. The average woman worker will work outside the home between _____ in her lifetime
    a. 5-10 years
    b. 10-15 years
    c. 15-20 years
    d. 20-40 years

Answers follow.

ANSWERS

1. The number of women who work for pay some time during their lives is:

   (d) nine out of ten.

2. The percentage of women who worked because of economic need in 1985 was:

   (d) 67 percent. Most women work because they have to work. The myth that women work only to amuse themselves, or to buy luxuries for their families, is a very limiting one because it is used to justify keeping women in low-paying jobs. •

3. Married men with non-working wives and one or more children in 1985 made up:

   (d) 9.9 percent of all households. Families are changing rapidly in today's society. The high divorce rate is creating many single-parent families. Also, many people are choosing not to have any children or to remain single.

4. Women make up:

   (c) 44 percent of the total workforce.

5. In 1984 the median earnings for men and women who work full time were:

   (b) men-$23,218, women-$14,780. The gap between the earnings of men and women is narrowing very slowly. Many explanations for the gap are given, but one of the most prominent reasons is that women are concentrated in low-paying jobs. For example, secretaries, who are usually women, make much less than construction workers, who are mostly men.

6. In the past decade, three-fifths of the labor force increase has been among

   (a) women. Women from all backgrounds are entering the workforce.

7. In 1985 fully employed women high school graduates (with no college background) earned:

   (b) less than men who did not complete elementary school. If you look back to the graph you completed earlier on page 39, you will see the large difference in the pay for traditional men's jobs versus traditional women's jobs. Notice that jobs such as house painter and truck driver are relatively high-salaried jobs even though they require little education. Construction or farm jobs often require apprenticeship or on-the-job training, rather than formal education.

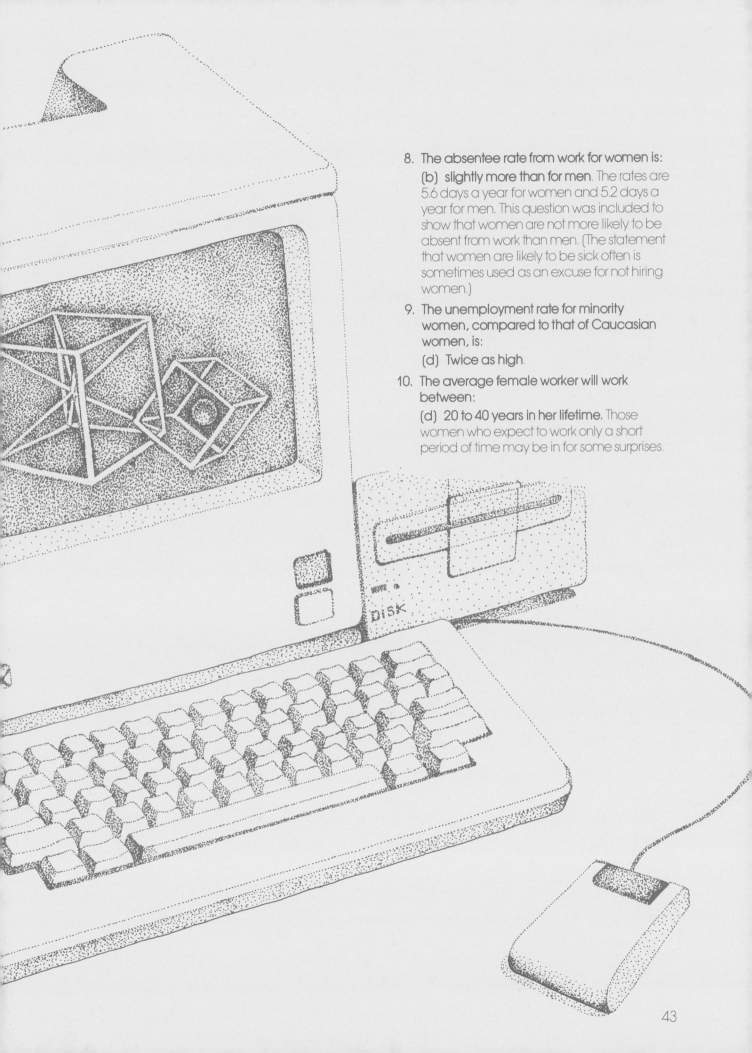

8. The absentee rate from work for women is:

    (b) **slightly more than for men.** The rates are 5.6 days a year for women and 5.2 days a year for men. This question was included to show that women are not more likely to be absent from work than men. (The statement that women are likely to be sick often is sometimes used as an excuse for not hiring women.)

9. The unemployment rate for minority women, compared to that of Caucasian women, is:

    (d) Twice as high.

10. The average female worker will work between:

    (d) **20 to 40 years in her lifetime.** Those women who expect to work only a short period of time may be in for some surprises.

REFLECTIONS

CHAPTER THREE

The High Cost of Living

Could you support a family
on your income alone?

The making of money is not a
sex-linked skill. Women can and
are turning it all around. We are
discovering for ourselves the
challenge — and the joy — of money.
— Paula Nelson
   Economist

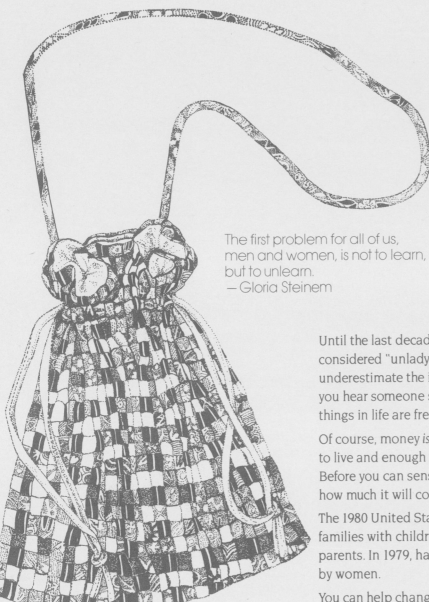

The first problem for all of us,
men and women, is not to learn,
but to unlearn.
— Gloria Steinem

Until the last decade, a concern for making money was considered "unladylike." Even today, women seem inclined to underestimate the importance of financial independence. When you hear someone say, "Money isn't everything" or "The best things in life are free," it's usually a woman.

Of course, money *isn't* everything. But having an adequate place to live and enough to eat certainly makes life more pleasant. Before you can sensibly decide on a career, you should know how much it will cost to live in a way that you will find pleasing.

The 1980 United States Census showed that 19.1 percent of families with children under age 18 were headed by single parents. In 1979, half of all poor families were maintained by women.

You can help change this gloomy picture.

It's not easy to break away from tradition. Even though millions of women — including married women and women with young children — are now working outside the home, women are still less likely than men to prepare seriously for a career.

See for yourself. Ask some of your friends, both male and female, what they were planning to do when they left school and what they are doing now. Be sure to interview both men and women and compare.

Interview

Name _____ Age _____ M or F _____

What were you planning to do after school? _____
_____
_____
_____

What are you doing now?
_____
_____
_____
_____

Name _____ Age _____ M or F _____

What were you planning to do after school? _____
_____
_____
_____

What are you doing now?
_____
_____
_____

Name _____ Age _____ M or F _____

What were you planning to do after school? _____
_____
_____
_____

What are you doing now?
_____
_____
_____
_____

Name _____ Age _____ M or F _____

What were you planning to do after school? _____

_____

_____

_____

What are you doing now?

_____

_____

_____

_____

Name _____ Age _____ M or F _____

What were you planning to do after school? _____

_____

_____

_____

What are you doing now?

_____

_____

_____

_____

Name _____ Age _____ M or F _____

What were you planning to do after school? _____

_____

_____

_____

What are you doing now?

_____

_____

_____

_____

Do you see patterns emerging for the men and women? If so, what are they?

True Stories: Could This Happen to You?

Remember, we're all in this alone.
— Lily Tomlin

You see "The Happily Ever After Story" dozens of times a week on TV. There may be a few problems and a few hilarious complications, but by the end of the hour, the hero says something witty or romantic, the heroine falls into his arms, the music swells and the credits begin to roll. Unfortunately, life does not come equipped with background music, a laugh track, or even a script. Anything can happen.

You may be — or plan to become — a full-time wife and mother who is supported by a husband. Just the same, your future will be more secure if you have the ability to support yourself, should the need arise. The following stories represent only a few of the situations for women today. Read them, and then jot down your reactions to the circumstances described. Indicate how common you think the situations are.

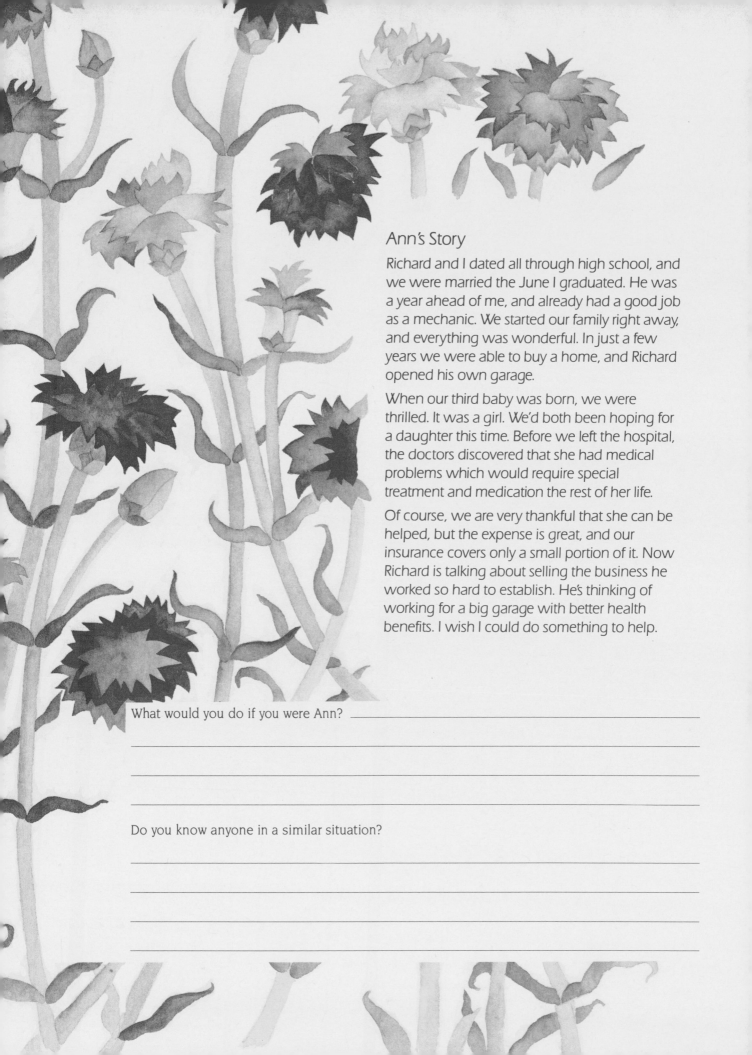

Ann's Story

Richard and I dated all through high school, and we were married the June I graduated. He was a year ahead of me, and already had a good job as a mechanic. We started our family right away, and everything was wonderful. In just a few years we were able to buy a home, and Richard opened his own garage.

When our third baby was born, we were thrilled. It was a girl. We'd both been hoping for a daughter this time. Before we left the hospital, the doctors discovered that she had medical problems which would require special treatment and medication the rest of her life.

Of course, we are very thankful that she can be helped, but the expense is great, and our insurance covers only a small portion of it. Now Richard is talking about selling the business he worked so hard to establish. He's thinking of working for a big garage with better health benefits. I wish I could do something to help.

What would you do if you were Ann? _____

_____

_____

_____

Do you know anyone in a similar situation?

_____

_____

_____

_____

Maria's Story

Because Geraldo was such a good provider, I never worried about money. He loved his job, and was always making investments. I never really knew how much money we had, but he never complained about the credit card payments, so I bought whatever I liked for the children and for our home.

Who would have thought someone as full of life as Geraldo would have a fatal heart attack when he was just 42 years old? I couldn't believe it.

After the funeral, Geraldo's lawyer asked me to come in and talk about finances. The lawyer told me that a few months before his death Geraldo made some risky investments that lost money. He'd borrowed on his life insurance, and most of our savings were gone. The house is paid for, but I don't know how I'm going to get the kids through high school, let alone college. The only job I've ever had was working part-time in a clothing store, and that only paid the minimum wage.

Could what happened to Maria happen to you? _____

_____

_____

_____

Why or why not? _____

_____

_____

_____

Marilyn's Story

I had always planned to get married and live happily ever after. When I married Bill, I thought everything was perfect. I really enjoyed staying home and keeping house. I made little Christmas tree ornaments that sold at a boutique each year. When our children were born I decorated their rooms, went to all the play groups for them, read books about child care. The kids seemed to develop well and were very happy. I was happy and I thought Bill was too. We'd both decided that it was important for me to stay home and raise the kids.

Then, as the years went by, Bill seemed to change. He became dissatisfied with his job and his life. He said he was bored and that I was not a very interesting person. Then he said he wanted a divorce. I didn't know what to do.

Bill left us, and although I feel sad for him, I also feel cheated and angry. I thought I was doing the right things with my life. I had cared for Bill and the kids. Now what am I going to do? Bill quit his job so there's not much money coming in. I'll never make enough money to support us by selling Christmas tree ornaments.

Do you know anyone in a similar situation? _____

_____

_____

_____

_____

What could Marilyn do to help herself? _____

_____

_____

_____

Tracy's Story

I was a good student in high school and chose to go to a major university. I majored in English because it was fun for me. I liked reading literature, writing and discussing ideas. College was an exciting time, and I made many friends, including my husband, John. We were married right after I graduated. John earned a degree in business administration and started work with a restaurant chain. He worked his way up to a management position; everything was going well for us. We had two children, a nice house, and I was an active community volunteer.

Last year another company bought out the restaurant chain John worked for, and brought in their own management people. John is having a hard time finding another position. We're behind in our house payments and may lose our home. I wish I could get a reasonable job to help make ends meet. I never thought about having to work to earn money.

Do you know anyone in a similar situation?

_____

_____

_____

_____

Could this happen to you? _____

_____

_____

_____

_____

Why or why not? _____

_____

_____

_____

_____

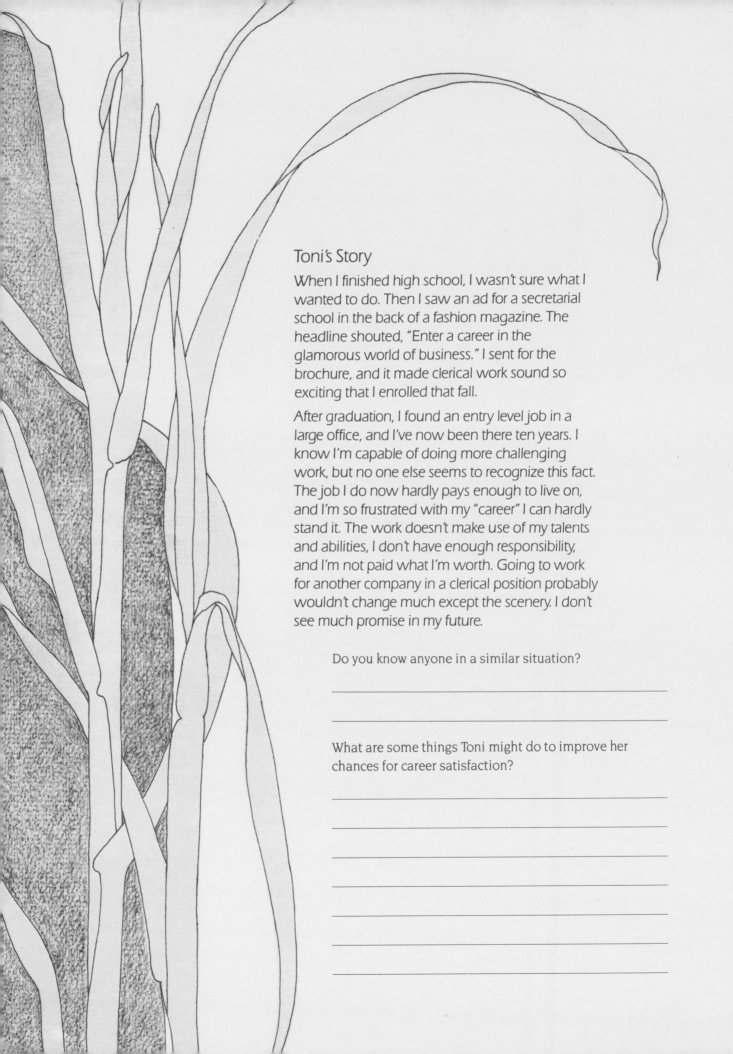

Toni's Story

When I finished high school, I wasn't sure what I wanted to do. Then I saw an ad for a secretarial school in the back of a fashion magazine. The headline shouted, "Enter a career in the glamorous world of business." I sent for the brochure, and it made clerical work sound so exciting that I enrolled that fall.

After graduation, I found an entry level job in a large office, and I've now been there ten years. I know I'm capable of doing more challenging work, but no one else seems to recognize this fact. The job I do now hardly pays enough to live on, and I'm so frustrated with my "career" I can hardly stand it. The work doesn't make use of my talents and abilities, I don't have enough responsibility, and I'm not paid what I'm worth. Going to work for another company in a clerical position probably wouldn't change much except the scenery. I don't see much promise in my future.

Do you know anyone in a similar situation?

_____

_____

What are some things Toni might do to improve her chances for career satisfaction?

_____

_____

_____

_____

_____

_____

_____

Think about yourself and the women you know. Have any of you faced problems similar to the ones you've just examined? What decisions have you had to make? What actions have you taken?

Write one of your stories in the space below.

If it's someone else's story, interview that person and write from her point of view.

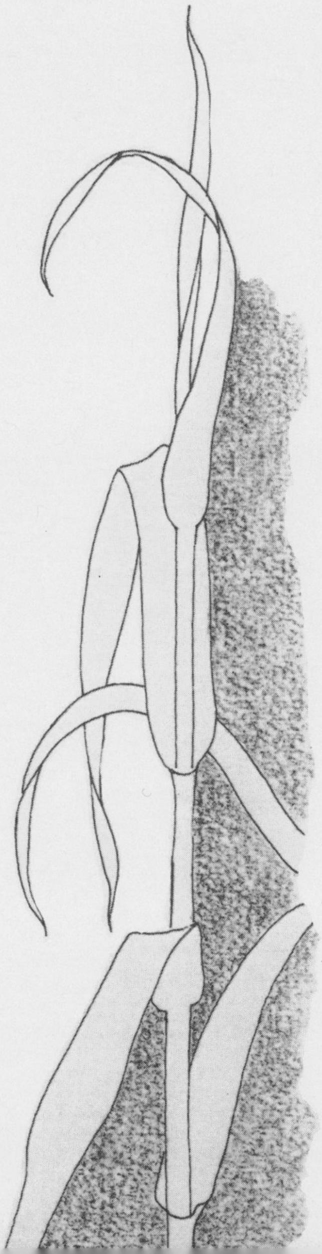

_____'s story:

_____

_____

_____

_____

_____

_____

_____

_____

_____

_____

_____

_____

_____

_____

_____

_____

_____

No one knows what the future holds. Expectations don't always materialize. If your expectations of a bright, secure future are to be fulfilled, it's important for you to be aware of your options for achieving them. Great expectations for the future should include several possible paths to security and happiness.

It's important to have a plan for financially supporting yourself at a level that will make you happy. If you have children or other dependents, you need to be able to support them, as well. Your ideal lifestyle doesn't have to include big houses and fancy cars, though it might. Give the subject some thought. Some people enjoy a modest lifestyle, while others have more expensive fantasies. It's your life, so try to think of what would please you. In the following exercise, you will make up a detailed budget to show how much money you need to earn to support your ideal way of life and, at the same time, be economically self-sufficient.

As you write your budget, whether you are married or not, assume that you are single. This budget should reflect what you need to be economically self-sufficient. If you have children now, assume that they will be your financial responsibility. If you plan to have children within the next ten years, pretend that you have them now for the sake of this exercise. List their sex and age below.

Number of children ____

Sex(es) ____ ____ ____ ____

Age(s) ____ ____ ____ ____

You are probably already aware of costs for many of the items you will be asked to consider. But you may have to do some research, too, especially if you are not now responsible for your family's finances. Some prices can be found in the classified ads of your local newspaper (especially prices for houses, apartments, cars). Whenever possible get the actual figures for your family.

YOU MAY BE TEMPTED TO SKIP THIS EXERCISE.
DON'T!
IT'S VERY IMPORTANT.

1. Housing

If you currently have housing that you find appealing, enter the monthly costs on page 65.

If your ideal lifestyle as the sole support of yourself, or yourself and your family, would require you to change your residence, work through the following exercise.

Whether or not you want to have an apartment in the city, a suburban home, or a cabin in the country, housing will probably be your biggest single expense. To help you determine housing costs, let's compare monthly rental payments and the costs for purchasing a house. Then you can select one or the other. We will begin with a rental.

To select an apartment or home to rent, decide what your requirements are (number of bedrooms, location, pets accepted, and so forth). Then check the "Apartments for Rent" or "Homes for Rent" section of the classified ads in a newspaper. Compare features and prices before selecting one you think you would like.

In the space below, copy two or three classified ads offering housing that might be suitable. Circle the monthly payment listed.

IF YOU ALREADY OWN
YOUR HOME

Who carries the mortgage? _____

How much is it? _____

What is the interest rate? _____

What are the monthly payments? _____

What is the current market value of your home? _____

BUYING A HOME

If you are considering buying a home, turn to "Houses for Sale" in the classified advertisement section of a newspaper. A house of your own will be more expensive than an apartment. However, houses offer many advantages, such as having a home of your own, tax benefits, and a long-term investment. Pick out several houses in different price ranges that appeal to you. Cut out these ads and paste them below, circling the listed selling price.

Houses are very expensive items today. And buying a house is much different than making an ordinary purchase. You begin by saving well in advance toward a down payment on the house. It is usually about 20 percent of the purchase price. For example, for a $60,000 house you would have to pay $12,000 cash as a down payment.
($60,000 x .20 = $12,000)

To obtain the rest of the money you will need to get a mortgage loan from a bank. The bank will pay the seller the full price of the house (minus the down payment). You in turn must pay the bank monthly for usually 15 to 30 years. The bank will charge you a fee (interest) for lending you its money.

For this exercise, figure out what your monthly payment would be on one of the houses you have chosen. To do so, work through the procedures given in the next section. First read the procedure, including the example. Then, using the purchase price of the house you have chosen, insert the proper figures in the blanks provided. When you are finished you will have found the amount of your monthly payment. This tells you what it would cost you to live in the house. You can then compare the cost of buying a house with the cost of renting, and choose one or the other.

FINDING MONTHLY PAYMENTS
WHEN BUYING A HOUSE

1. Multiply the purchase price of your house by 20% (.20). The answer is the down payment you will have to pay.

2. Subtract the down payment from the purchase price. This gives you the amount you will need to borrow from the bank; that is, the amount of your loan.

Remember we said the bank will charge you interest for loaning you its money. Since this will be a major part of your monthly payment, you must figure the interest cost to find your total monthly payment. The bank does this by figuring out the number of thousands there are in your loan (dividing your loan by 1,000). For example, a $40,000 loan equals 40,000 ÷ 1,000 or 40 thousands. When a borrower agrees to a loan, the bank states the interest rate it will charge. The bank then computes the monthly payment using a standard table which lists the cost for each $1,000 of loan at different interest rates.

Look at the following table.

MONTHLY COST PER $1,000 OF LOAN

Rate of Interest	Dollars to be Paid for Each $1,000 Loan
8%	$ 7.34 for each $1,000
9%	$ 8.05 for each $1,000
10%	$ 8.78 for each $1,000
11%	$ 9.52 for each $1,000
12%	$10.29 for each $1,000
13%	$11.06 for each $1,000
14%	$11.85 for each $1,000
15%	$12.68 for each $1,000

Let's say you have a loan at 11 percent interest. This table states that *every month* you will have to pay $9.52 multiplied by the number of thousands in the loan.

EXAMPLE:
For a $40,000 loan at 11% interest, the payment would be:

40 x $9.52 = $381 per month.

When a borrower agrees to the loan, the bank states the interest rate it will charge.

To continue your calculation,

3. Divide the amount of the loan by 1,000. This provides the number of thousands in the loan.

4. Choose an interest rate from the chart. (In reality you must pay the rate the bank asks based on current loan rates.)

5. Multiply the dollars to be paid per thousand by the number of thousands in the loan. This gives the total monthly payment.

Now here's an example of the whole procedure.

EXAMPLE:

Beautiful three-bedroom, one-bath house on large lot.
Close to shopping and schools. Good financing. $100,000.
Call 654-8324.

Purchase price	$100,000
Multiplied by 20%	x .20
Equals down payment	$ 20,000
Amount of loan equals $100,000 minus $20,000	$ 80,000

There are 80 thousands in $80,000, (80,000 ÷ 1,000). If your interest rate is 11 percent, multiply the rate per thousand shown in the table for 11 percent. That is 9.52 times 80, which is the number of thousands in your loan.

Amount per thousand	$ 9.52
Multiplied by 80	x 80
Equals monthly payment	$761.60

Okay, now it is time for you to try it.

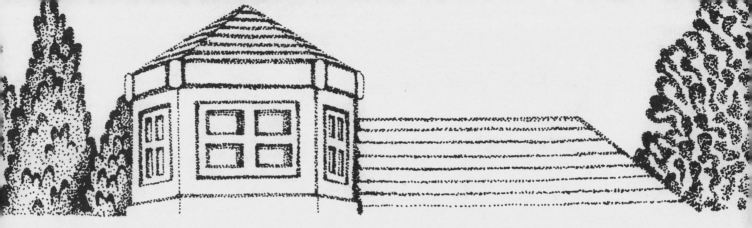

The purchase price of the home I would like to buy is $_____ .

1. Multiply the purchase price by .20 to get the down payment.

    Purchase price $ _____

    Multiplied by 20%   x   .20

    Equals down payment $ _____

2. Subtract down payment from the
    purchase price.

    Purchase price $ _____

    Minus down payment $ _____

    Equals loan $ _____

3. Divide the amount of your loan by 1,000.

    Loan $ _____

    Divided by 1,000   ÷ 1,000

    Equals number of
    thousands   _____

4. Choose an amount from the interest rate
    table on page 59.

    At _____% interest the amount per thousand is _____.

5. Multiply the amount per $1,000 by the
    number of thousands in your loan.

    Amount per thousand $ _____

    Multiplied by
    number of thousands   _____

    EQUALS MONTHLY PAYMENT   _____

Now we've figured the cost of buying a home, right? Not yet! There are two other costs we must add. These are taxes and homeowner's insurance — neither of which renters have to pay.

Every state collects property taxes from homeowners. An approximate tax, using California as an example, is 1 percent of the assessed value. "Assessed value" refers to the amount the state thinks your house is worth. When you buy a house, the assessed value is usually the same as the purchase price. To figure your monthly taxes, multiply the purchase price by 1 percent; or find your state's formula for charging property taxes.

Purchase price $ _____

Multiplied by 1%   x   .01
or your state's multiple

Equals yearly property tax $ _____

To find monthly cost, divide yearly
property tax by 12.

Taxes $ _____ per month.

When you get a home loan, the bank will require you to have homeowner's insurance. Some sample yearly insurance payments (known as premiums) are listed below. Find the premium that is closest to the purchase price you chose, and divide the yearly premium by 12. This will tell you how much your insurance will actually cost each month, even though it's not paid by the month.

Sample Yearly Premiums
($100 deductible coverage)

$ 80,000 - $234/year
$ 90,000 - $268/year
$100,000 - $300/year
$120,000 - $359/year
$150,000 - $444/year

Homeowner's Insurance $ _____ per month.

Your monthly homeowner's expenses will be:

Monthly payment $ _____

Monthly property taxes $ _____

Monthly homeowner's insurance $ _____

TOTAL MONTHLY COST OF A HOUSE
(Add payment, taxes,
and insurance.) $ _____

Your monthly payment for the apartment you are considering would be:

MONTHLY RENT $ _____

Did you choose the apartment to rent or the house to buy? Write your choice below. What are the reasons for your choice?

_____

_____

_____

_____

_____

_____

_____

_____

_____

_____

_____

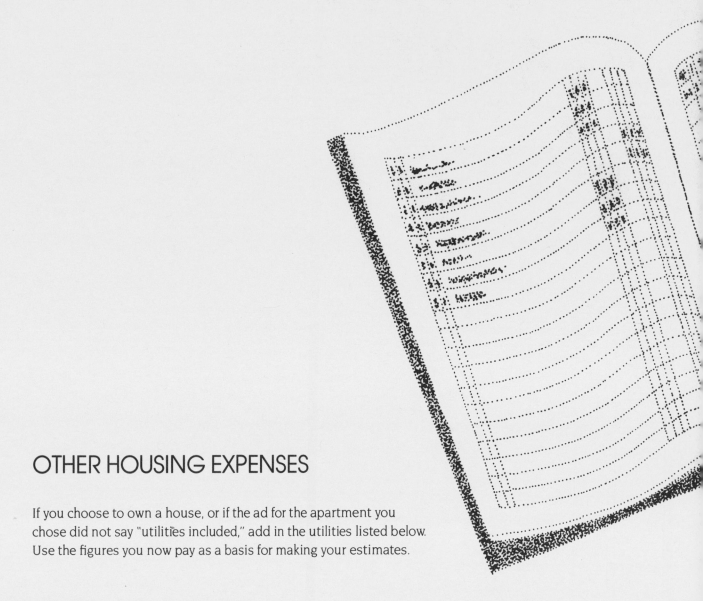

OTHER HOUSING EXPENSES

If you choose to own a house, or if the ad for the apartment you chose did not say "utilities included," add in the utilities listed below. Use the figures you now pay as a basis for making your estimates.

UTILITIES

Gas	$ _____	per month
Electricity	$ _____	per month
Water	$ _____	per month
Garbage	$ _____	per month
Sewer	$ _____	per month
TOTAL UTILITIES	$ _____	per month
Telephone	$ _____	per month

Don't forget to budget for long distance calls.

If you expect to have cable TV or special television, determine the cost by calling the local television company.

Cable TV	$ _____	per month

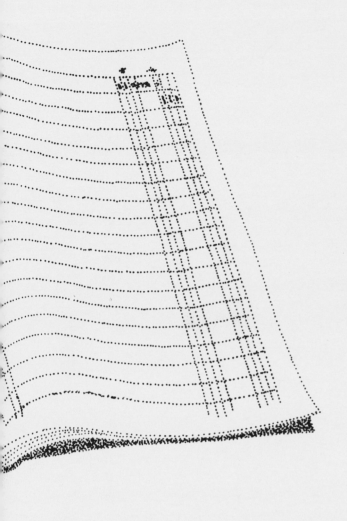

In 1985 average monthly utility bills in four cities[5] were approximately as shown here.*

Los Angeles	$ 82
Houston	$ 87
New York	$151
Kansas City	$ 98

To find your total housing costs, add the items listed below.

MONTHLY RENT OR HOMEOWNER'S EXPENSES

Total monthly cost of residence
(house or rental) $ _____

Total utilities $ _____

Phone $ _____

Cable TV $ _____

TOTAL HOUSING COSTS $ _____ [1]

Enter at (1) in Your Monthly Budget on page 79.

*We have included average figures at times in this budget exercise to give you a starting point for your estimates. The averages are approximate and are not meant to be used as totally accurate portrayals of today's costs. The amounts involved in budgeting make finding your true costs extremely difficult without taking particular circumstances into account. Utilities, for example, vary according to geographical location, type and size of house, amount of insulation, number of residents, etc. In addition, rising prices may make our estimates too low by the time you read them.

2. Transportation

A few cities offer adequate public transportation, but most people want a car. Whether it's a shiny new sports car or an old jalopy, paying for it and keeping it running will take a sizeable portion of your monthly income.

Describe a car you currently have, or one you would like to buy, in the space below.

Let's assume that you have found a car that should serve you well. Let's also assume you don't have enough money to pay the full price in cash, but you do have enough for a down payment. After making a down payment, you could get a loan to help pay for the car. Then you would have to make a series of monthly payments. So the next big question is: Can you afford the monthly payments on top of the day to day costs of owning a car? In the table which follows, find the amount closest to the price for the car you chose, and write the monthly payment in the space below the table.

If you finance for 48 months (48 payments):

Loan Amount	Monthly payments		
	16% annual interest	12% annual interest	8% annual interest
$3,000	$ 85	$ 79	$ 73
$5,000	$141	$131	$122
$7,000	$198	$184	$171
$9,000	$255	$237	$220

Monthly payment $ _____

Can you afford monthly payments in addition to the cost of running the car you chose? You will need to buy gasoline. The approximate monthly cost of gasoline can be found by the following procedure.

Estimate the number of miles you might drive per week. Consider:
— Back and forth to work.
— Trips to children's school or daycare center.
— Trips to the store.
— Visits.
— Weekend driving.

EXAMPLE
If Jane drives a small Honda she might get 30 miles to the gallon around town. Her work place is 5 miles from her home, so she drives at least 10 miles a day (5 days a week). Dropping kids off at the babysitter takes another 4 miles a day round trip (5 days a week). Shopping and errands account for another 30 miles a week. On the weekends she averages about 60 miles. Her total mileage is around 150 miles per week. At 30 miles to the gallon Jane needs:

$150 \div 30 = 5$ gallons of gas per week,
or 5 gallons multiplied by the price per gallon.

EXAMPLE
$ .89 per gallon equals
$.89
x 5
$4.45 per week
 x 4 weeks equals $17.80 per month.

Now repeat the calculations with your figures.

Your estimated number of miles per week: _____

Determine the number of miles your car will go on one gallon of gasoline (car dealers or people you know have that information). Remember that estimates in car ads are usually much higher than you will actually get.

Estimated miles per gallon (mpg) _____

Divide the number of miles driven per week by the mpg.

Multiply the number of gallons per week you use by the current price of gasoline per gallon. This will give you the cost of gasoline for a week. To find monthly costs, multiply the weekly cost by four.

Gasoline cost per month $ _____

Every car needs tune-ups, oil and filter changes, and a certain amount of regular maintenance. Tires wear out, and the life of a battery is about three to five years. All these things add to the cost of driving a car. Such costs vary by the size and the complexity of the car. Nevertheless, you can get a rough average by knowing how many cylinders a car's engine has. Choose the monthly average for your car from the list that follows.

Engine cylinders	4	6	8
Average maintenance cost per month	$18	$24	$30

Monthly car maintenance $ _____

Yearly car expenses also include registration or license plate renewal and insurance. Some states only charge a registration fee each year, but others, such as California, include a property tax in the annual license fee. Where this is the case, renewal will be costly for an expensive car, but quite cheap for an old car. If your car is financed, the loan company will require you to have insurance to pay for the car if it is damaged or stolen. If you own your car outright, you can reduce insurance costs by not buying collision insurance. If you make this choice, however, you'll get no help in repairing your car if you have an accident. As you can see, license and insurance costs vary, so your best bet is to ask locally to find out what they would be.

After you have learned the license and insurance costs per year, add them together and divide the total by 12 months to get the cost per month.

Yearly costs:

Car license (expiration date _____) $ _____

Insurance (policy # _____) $ _____

Total yearly costs: $ _____

Costs per month (divide by 12): $ _____

As an alternative to owning a car, public transportation may be available to you. Multiply the cost of one bus, subway, or train ride by the expected number of rides in one month.

Public transportation cost
per month: $ _____

To find your total transportation costs,
add the following items.

Monthly car payments $ _____

Gasoline $ _____

Car maintenance $ _____

License and insurance $ _____

Public transportation $ _____

TOTAL TRANSPORTATION COSTS $ _____ [2]

Enter at (2) in "Your Monthly Budget" on page 79.

3. Clothing

For the purpose of this exercise, assume that you already have a basic wardrobe; you only need to replace items or purchase new clothes that you want. And, if you have children, they will need clothes too.

To find your monthly clothing costs under your ideal budget, first determine the number of purchases you would like to make in a year for each clothing category.

For example, how many new dresses would you like to buy in a year?

Number of dresses _____

Multiply the number of dresses you will purchase in a year by the average cost of a dress. Do the same for the other items listed below. Then add your totals to get your grand total for a year.

	Number of Purchases	x	Average Cost		TOTAL
Dresses	_____	x	$ _____	=	$ _____
Skirts	_____	x	$ _____	=	$ _____
Tops	_____	x	$ _____	=	$ _____
Pants	_____	x	$ _____	=	$ _____
Coats	_____	x	$ _____	=	$ _____
Bathing suit	_____	x	$ _____	=	$ _____
Pajamas	_____	x	$ _____	=	$ _____
Underwear	_____	x	$ _____	=	$ _____
Shoes	_____	x	$ _____	=	$ _____
Miscellaneous	_____	x	$ _____	=	$ _____

GRAND TOTAL
for a year $ _____

Divide the grand total by twelve to learn the monthly average for your clothing expenses.

Grand total $ _____ divided by 12 equals:

TOTAL COST PER MONTH $ _____

Children

If you have children or expect to have children, figure the cost of clothing for each child. Be sure to consider their ages and the fact that they will not have much they can use from the previous year.

BOY	Number of Purchases	x	Average Cost		TOTAL
Pants	_____	x	$ _____	=	$ _____
Shirts	_____	x	$ _____	=	$ _____
Shoes	_____	x	$ _____	=	$ _____
Underwear	_____	x	$ _____	=	$ _____
Socks	_____	x	$ _____	=	$ _____
Jackets	_____	x	$ _____	=	$ _____
Shorts	_____	x	$ _____	=	$ _____
Bathing suit	_____	x	$ _____	=	$ _____
Miscellaneous	_____	x	$ _____	=	$ _____
			GRAND TOTAL		$ _____

Grand total $ _____ divided by 12 equals:

TOTAL COST PER MONTH $ _____

GIRL	Number of Purchases	x	Average Cost		TOTAL
Dresses	_____	x	$ _____	=	$ _____
Pants	_____	x	$ _____	=	$ _____
Tops	_____	x	$ _____	=	$ _____
Coats, jackets	_____	x	$ _____	=	$ _____
Shoes, boots	_____	x	$ _____	=	$ _____
Bathing suit	_____	x	$ _____	=	$ _____
Pajamas	_____	x	$ _____	=	$ _____
Underwear	_____	x	$ _____	=	$ _____
Miscellaneous	_____	x	$ _____	=	$ _____
			GRAND TOTAL		$ _____

Grand total $ _____ divided by 12 equals

TOTAL COST PER MONTH $ _____

Add up all the monthly figures for you and your children to find your total clothing costs.

Your clothing $ _____

Child $ _____

Child $ _____

TOTAL CLOTHING COSTS PER MONTH $ _____ [3]

Enter at (3) in "Your Monthly Budget" on page 79.

4. Food

Use the amount that your family spends on food each week to estimate the cost of feeding your family. If you want to change your eating habits, estimate the costs. When you make your estimate, remember to include non-food items usually bought at the grocery store. Things like detergent, paper goods, cosmetics, vitamins, and notions add greatly to the average "food" bill.

Estimate your weekly cost and multiply the total by 4 to reach a monthly figure.

Food bill per week $ _____

Multiply by 4   _____ x 4

Monthly cost $ _____

**TOTAL FOOD COSTS
PER MONTH** $ _____ [4]

Enter at (4) in "Your Monthly Budget" on page 79.

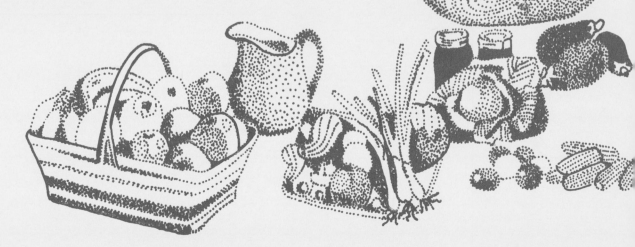

The table you see here shows some average food costs for a woman and two children in April 1986. The figures reflect only the cost of food items. The cost of food items is approximately 80 percent of the total grocery store bill. Again, keep in mind that these amounts are only approximate and subject to much variation.

SAMPLE FOOD COSTS[6]

	Thrifty	Low	Moderate	Liberal
Per week	$ 37	$ 46	$ 57	$ 70
Per month	$149	$186	$227	$280

5. Entertainment

Life would be dull if you could only spend money on things that are absolutely necessary. What do you do for fun? Concerts? Movies? Skiing? If you have children, what kinds of opportunities do you want to provide for them? Do you want them to have dance or music lessons, horseback-riding lessons, to be Scouts, or participate in sports?

Hobbies can be expensive. Do you like to play tennis or raquetball, or to participate in similar activities? Will you want a membership in an athletic club, golf, swim or tennis club? What about buying and maintaining a boat, a hang glider or a horse?

If you would like to take a vacation, you will probably need to save for it. Let's say you want to rent a cabin which costs $360 per week. If so, you would need to save $30 a month for a year to afford one week's rental.

Describe how you would spend your entertainment dollar in your ideal lifestyle.

Movies, concerts, etc.	$ _____ per month
Restaurants	$ _____ per month
Children's entertainment and memberships	$ _____ per month
Vacation	$ _____ per month
Hobbies	$ _____ per month
Other entertainment	$ _____ per month
TOTAL ENTERTAINMENT COSTS	$ _____ [5] per month

Enter at (5) in "Your Monthly Budget" on page 79.

6. Furnishings

You will probably need to buy some items for your apartment, house or yard. Assume for this exercise that you already have some basic furniture and furnishings. In your estimate, include only additional purchases, such as linens, plants and decorations. This budget category should also carry some emergency funds to cover unexpected repairs. You'll be glad you set the money aside when the refrigerator fails or you need to replace a hot water heater.

TOTAL FURNISHING COSTS PER MONTH $ _____ [6]

Enter at (6) in "Your Monthly Budget" on page 79.

7. Health Care

Most health care costs are paid by employers as benefits, or "extras" above and beyond wages. However, there are still things left you'll have to pay for yourself.

To figure this cost, assume an employer pays your health insurance, but you pay pharmacy expenses and all doctors' bills less than $100.

Also include in this section the costs of dental bills, glasses, braces, and some drug store articles.

Average health care costs for a family of three might be around $110 per month.

TOTAL HEALTH CARE PER MONTH $ _____ [7]

Enter at (7) in "Your Monthly Budget" on page 79.

Remember to include saving for major, unexpected health problems in your savings section (section nine, upcoming). You can never tell when you or your child will have an acute case of appendicitis, fall off a bike and break an arm, or suffer from a chronic illness.

8. Child Care

If you work and have a child, your child will probably need child care. For example, a five-year-old would need care before or after half-day kindergarten. You will also need to estimate the cost of babysitters for times when you would like to go out alone. Such times should be added to your total child care costs.

If you don't already have children, make your estimate checking with local daycare facilities to get sample costs, or figure from the hourly rate charged for babysitting.

Total number of hours of care per week		_____
Multiplied by cost per hour	$	_____
Equals cost per week	$	_____

To find the cost per month, multiply the cost per week by four.   _____ x 4

TOTAL CHILD CARE COSTS PER MONTH $ _____ [8]

Enter at (8) in "Your Monthly Budget" on page 79.

9. Savings

How would you like to have a video cassette recorder or take a trip? To buy special things you will probably need to save some money from your paycheck. You also need to think about, and be prepared for, unexpected expenses, like medical bills or a leaky roof. Do you want to send your kids to college? What about retirement? Select a reasonable amount to save each month and write it below.

TOTAL SAVINGS COSTS PER MONTH $ _____ [9]

Where is your savings account?   _____

Enter at (9) in "Your Monthly Budget" on page 79.

10. Miscellaneous

Toys $ _____ per month

Gifts $ _____ per month

Pets $ _____ per month

Anything else $ _____ per month

TOTAL MISCELLANEOUS COSTS
PER MONTH $ _____ [10]

Enter at (10) in "Your Monthly Budget" on page 79.

Sample Budget

A reasonable budget for a woman with two children living in Dallas, Texas during 1987 might look something like the following.

MONTHLY BUDGET

Housing		
Buying	$ 650	
Renting		$ 350
Transportation	$ 220	
Clothing	$ 115	
Food	$ 280	
Entertainment	$ 50	
Furnishings	$ 50	
Health care	$ 110	
Child care	$ 200	
Savings	$ 50	
Miscellaneous	$ 25	
TOTAL	$1750	$1450

Your Monthly Budget

To determine your total monthly expenses, use the lines you see here to record the amount you arrived at for each preceding numbered section. Adding up all these figures will give you the total amount you can expect to spend in a month, according to your ideal budget.

MONTHLY BUDGET

Housing	(1)	$ _____
Transportation	(2)	$ _____
Clothing	(3)	$ _____
Food	(4)	$ _____
Entertainment	(5)	$ _____
Furnishings	(6)	$ _____
Health care	(7)	$ _____
Child care	(8)	$ _____
Savings	(9)	$ _____
Miscellaneous	(10)	$ _____
TOTAL		$ _____

One More Step

Remember that, to have enough money to spend, you will need to earn more than the amount you came up with for your budget. The salary offered when you apply for a job is *gross pay,*. The *gross pay* is the salary before taxes and other assessments are subtracted. Money will be withheld for Social Security, and state and federal income taxes. Additional amounts for pensions, benefits, or contributions may also be withheld.

Let's assume in this exercise that an average percentage for withholding is 20 percent. This means that if your gross pay is $1,600 a month, you will only take home $1,280. This take-home pay or *net pay* is the money you will be able to spend. The amount you found you would need when you completed your budget should be equal to, or less than, the *net pay* you will take home.

To find the salary you will need to cover the expenses as determined in your budget, divide your monthly net pay by 80 percent.

80% of Gross Pay = Net Pay

Gross Pay = Net Pay divided by .80

EXAMPLE
If your monthly expenses were $1,000 then you would need to earn $1,250 per month in gross pay.

X = Gross Pay
Net Pay = $1,000
80% of X = $1,000
X = 1,000 divided by .80
X = $1,250

To find the yearly net salary you will need, multiply your monthly net salary by 12. You can figure the yearly gross salary needed by substituting the monthly gross salary for the monthly net salary, and multiplying by twelve months.

CONVERTING HOURLY SALARIES TO YEARLY SALARIES

There are 52 weeks per year and the average full-time job is 40 hours per week.

52 weeks a year x 40 hours per week = 2,080 hours per year

2,080 hours per year x $_____ salary per hour = $_____ salary for one year.

EXAMPLES
2,080 hours/year x $ 4/hour = $ 8,320/year
2,080 hours/year x $ 5/hour = $10,400/year
2,080 hours/year x $ 6/hour = $12,480/year
2,080 hours/year x $10/hour = $20,800/year
2,080 hours/year x $15/hour = $31,200/year
2,080 hours/year x $20/hour = $41,600/year

Looking for Work

That's it. You've finally arrived at the minimum salary you'll need to earn to support your family in the way you'd like. Now you need to find a job that will pay you that salary. Here are some examples of what other women found when they completed the budget exercise.

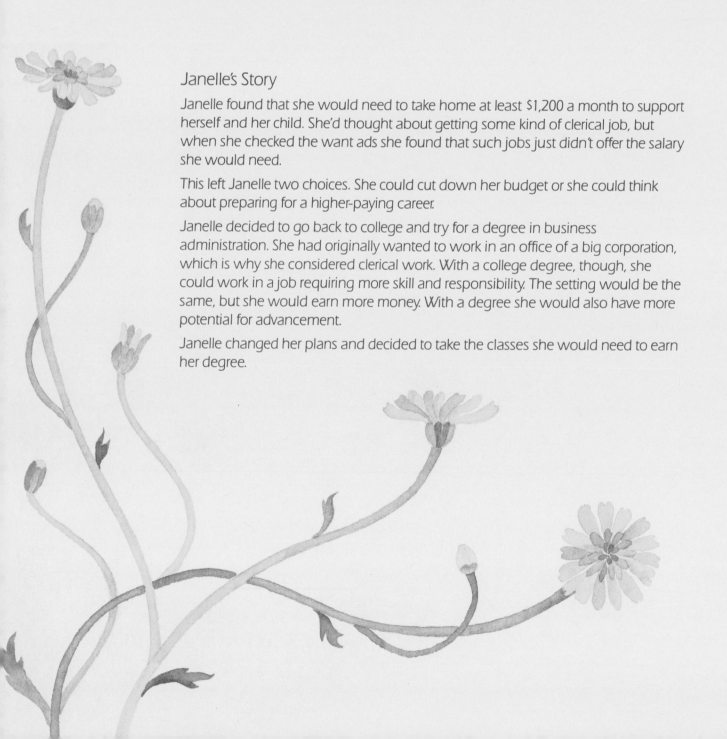

Janelle's Story

Janelle found that she would need to take home at least $1,200 a month to support herself and her child. She'd thought about getting some kind of clerical job, but when she checked the want ads she found that such jobs just didn't offer the salary she would need.

This left Janelle two choices. She could cut down her budget or she could think about preparing for a higher-paying career.

Janelle decided to go back to college and try for a degree in business administration. She had originally wanted to work in an office of a big corporation, which is why she considered clerical work. With a college degree, though, she could work in a job requiring more skill and responsibility. The setting would be the same, but she would earn more money. With a degree she would also have more potential for advancement.

Janelle changed her plans and decided to take the classes she would need to earn her degree.

Susan's Story

When Susan, newly widowed, completed her ideal budget she was amazed to find that she would need nearly $1,400 per month to live and support her two children. After the death of her father, Susan had watched her mother struggle to pay the monthly bills. To do it, her mother had to work many hours of overtime at the local shop where she clerked.

Susan had originally thought she would be a dental assistant. But when she researched how much it paid, she changed her plans and decided to become a dental technician instead. Although it meant more sacrifice now (more studying, less time for herself), and more years in school, Susan knew from her mother's experience that the ability to support a family was necessary for her peace of mind.

Cheryl's Story

Cheryl's mother always said, "You need to have a career you can fall back on in case you're ever a widow and have to support a family." Her mother's message hit home and Cheryl always knew that she wanted that type of insurance.

Cheryl graduated from college with a degree in computer science and then worked for an international computer company. Two years later, Cheryl married. Shortly thereafter she started a family. Cheryl's husband had a good job with an investment firm, so Cheryl changed to minimal part time at work and spent most of her time being a mother.

When the children were five and two years old, Cheryl's husband started drinking. Before long, he was drinking himself into a drunken stupor by early evening—every evening. Cheryl, the relatives, her husband's business associates and the family doctor tried everything they could to get him to stop. Life at home was becoming unbearable. One evening Cheryl returned home after visiting a sick relative in the hospital, to find her husband raging drunkenly and yelling about how the children wouldn't stop crying. She found the baby screaming in her crib with welts obviously inflicted by a belt. Her five-year-old was hiding in the closet, bruised and afraid to come out.

Cheryl picked up the children, walked out of the house, and within a week had an apartment, an attorney and a full-time job that would support her family. Cheryl's earlier career planning gave her the option of making the best decisions for her children and allowed her to be a strong and protective mother.

Now Find a Job

As you can see from the preceding example, it pays to think about your future.

What kind of work will you be qualified to do? For information on jobs, how much they pay, and what kinds of skills they require, you might consult:

1. The classified advertising section of your local newspaper.
2. The classified advertising section of a major newspaper from the nearest city of over 500,000 people.
3. The *Occupational Outlook Handbook*, written by the U.S. Department of Labor, which is available in libraries. (A list of sample jobs and job salaries from the *Occupational Outlook Handbook* is included on the following page.)
4. A Career Center, if one is available.

Select a job you think you will be qualified for and write the job title and salary in the space provided.

Title _____ Salary _____

Will this job enable you to live the way you want?

To qualify for the job you have chosen, how should you prepare?

Copy three or four employment ads from the classified section below.

What other sources of income do you have? How much per month?

That amount can be added to your monthly earned income figure.

Alimony? _____ Investment income? _____

Child support? _____ Interest income? _____

Other? _____

SAMPLE LIST OF JOBS AND SALARIES*

Architect	$29,000 (1984)
Artist (Graphic)	$19,000 (1984)
Automobile Body Repairer	$29,000 (1984)
Automobile Mechanic	$26,000 (1984)
Bank Teller	$11,000 (1984)
Bus Driver (Inter-city)	$24,000 (1984)
Buyer	$20,000 (1984)
Cashier (Union)	$23,000 (1984)
Chemist	$34,000 (1984)
Computer Programmer	$26,000 (1984)
Computer Service Technician	$25,000 (1984)
Cosmetologist	$17,000 (1984)
Dancer	Usually paid by performance. Work is often irregular.
Dental Assistant	$12,000 (1984)
Designer	$22,000 (1984)
Dietician	$28,000 (1984)
Economist	$29,000 (1984)
Electrician	$23,000 (1984)
Engineer	$41,000 (1985)
Flight Attendant	$23,000 (1984)
Forester	$31,000 (1984)
Hotel Manager	$30,000 (1983)
Lawyer	$88,000 (1984)
Legal Assistant	$20,000 (1984)
Mail Carrier	$25,000 (1985)
Nurse	$21,000 (1984)
Photographer	$24,000 (1984)
Physician	$108,000 (1984)
Physical Therapist	$25,000 (1985)
Pilot	$80,000 (1984)
Plumber	$21,000 (1984)
Police Officer (Patrol)	$21,000 (1984)
Principal (Senior High)	$42,000 (1984-85)
Principal (Junior High)	$40,000 (1984-85)
Principal (Elementary)	$37,000 (1984-85)
Psychologist (Ph.D.)	$36,000 (1983)
Receptionist	$14,000 (1985)
Recreation Worker	$19,000 (1984)
Sales Clerk (Retail)	$15,000 (1984)
Securities Sales Worker	$64,000 (1984)
School Counselor	$28,000 (1984-85)
Social Worker (MSW)	$26,000 (1984)
Sociologist	$32,000 (1983)
Teacher (Secondary)	$24,000 (1984-85)
Teacher (Elementary)	$23,000 (1984-85)
Telephone Operator	$15,000 (1984)
Tool and Die Maker	$23,000 (1984)
Typist	$15,000 (1984)
Welder	$27,000 (1984)

* All figures are given to the nearest thousands. The amounts shown are averages. These figures are average figures subject to many variations in individual circumstances. In some cases, annual figures have been computed from hourly wages, based on a 40 hour work week for a full year. Actual work hours may differ, causing inaccuracies in the annual salaries listed.

REFLECTIONS

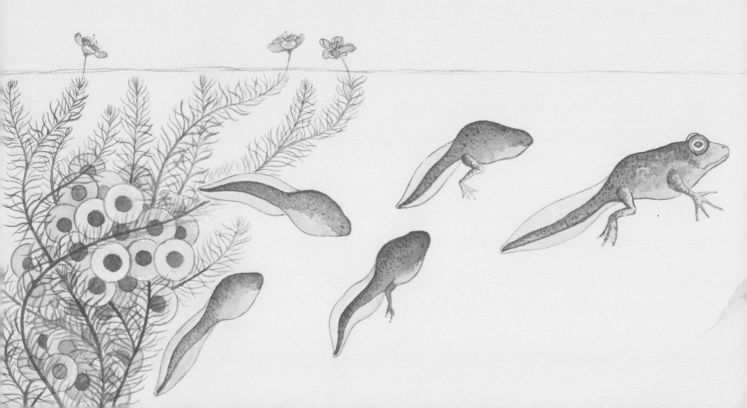

CHAPTER FOUR

Knowing What You Want Out of Life

Values and goal setting

You have to know exactly what you want out of your career. If you want to be a star, you don't bother with other things.
— Marilyn Horne
   Opera Singer

Whenever two good people argue over principles, they are both right.
— Marie Ebner von Eschenbach
   Austrian Author

Your Values

Before you can achieve any goals in life, you have to set them; and before you can wisely set them, you need to decide what is most important to you, and just how important it is.

Some of your possessions are more important than others. Some of your activities are more enjoyable, or more meaningful than others. If you were to state your goals for the future, some things would be at the top of the list and others far below. We use the term "values" to refer to all of the preceding, and more. Your personal values may place extra importance on possessions, religion, friendship, marriage, work, or any number of other things. Until you have a clear sense of what's important to you — your values — it will be difficult to make informed decisions about your future.

Esther's Story

Esther, for example, always assumed that she would become a nurse. Her mother was a nurse, and Esther grew up respecting the nursing profession. She was good at math and science, and had no trouble getting into nursing school.

Working in a hospital, though, made her unhappy. Esther enjoyed working alone, and the hospital was crowded and noisy, with half a dozen things going on at any given time in many of the rooms. Esther loved being outdoors, and hated the way her job kept her inside all day. At the end of her shift she was too exhausted to do anything else.

Esther decided to make a change. The fact that she was good at her job, she discovered, did not automatically mean that she was happy or satisfied with it. She had to consider her values, as well as her skills. What could she do, she wondered, that would make use of her math and science skills, while allowing her to be on her own and outdoors much of the time? After some searching, Esther had an answer: She decided to combine her math and science skills with her love of the outdoors by becoming a surveyor for the county. She has been much happier since.

Had Esther taken the time to consider her values before she made her initial career choice, she might easily have seen that nursing was not the best career for her. It's important for you to examine your values, too. Your values are reflected in the kinds of people you like and respect, your favorite activities, the places in which you feel most comfortable—in short, in how you react to the many different aspects of your life.

There are no right or wrong values when it comes to making a decision about a future career. You just need to be sure that they are *yours*, not those of your best friend, or the star of your favorite TV show.

The exercise that follows will help you determine what your values are right now. By taking a look at what you like to do, and why you like to do it, you may begin to learn some of the values that should play a part in your career choice.

WHAT DO I ENJOY DOING?

List 20 things you like to do, such as bike riding, entertaining, reading, playing tennis, writing, and so forth. Use the spaces provided under the word "Activities."

ACTIVITIES	1	2	3	4	5	6	7	8	9
1.									
2.									
3.									
4.									
5.									
6.									
7.									
8.									
9.									
10.									
11.									
12.									
13.									
14.									
15.									
16.									
17.									
18.									
19.									
20.									

To the right of each activity:

In column 1: write a **P** if the activity is usually done with people. Write an **A** if it is usually done alone.

In column 2: write a **$** if the activity costs more than $5.

In column 3: write an **O** if the activity is usually done outdoors. Write an **I** if it is usually done indoors.

In column 4: write an **M** if your mother would probably have the activity on her list.

In column 5: write an **H** if it is very important that your husband or future husband include this activity on his list.

In column 6: write an **O** if you now do this activity often, an **ST** if you do it sometimes, and an **R** if it is done rarely.

In column 7: write a **2** if you would have listed the activity two years ago.

In column 8: write an **A** if the activity requires you to be active physically. Write a **P** if the activity is physically passive.

In column 9: rank the **5** activities you like best, in the order of importance from **1** to **5** (1 = most important; 5 = least important).

Now examine the table to see if any themes or patterns are apparent in what you like to do. Is there a pattern in the underlying values too?

It's sad, but true: You can't have *everything* you want. All jobs have their unpleasant aspects, or at least a few that you will find less rewarding than others. The trick, then, is to choose a career that matches as *many* of your values as possible, especially those that are *most essential* to your happiness.

Margaret's Story

When she graduated from law school, Margaret was offered two jobs. The first was a high-paying position with a large firm in a big city. At this job, she would be doing research for the senior lawyers, and other tasks that she considered boring. The other job was with a law clinic in a rural area. Here she would receive less money, but she would have an opportunity to handle her own cases and to do work she considered important to society.

It was a difficult choice, but after carefully examining her values, Margaret decided to take the lower-paying position. She realized that it would mean leaving her friends, most of whom lived in the city, as well as having a job with less prestige. But she knew that to her, independence was more important than wealth or prestige.

What are your values? The following exercise will help you sort them out and it will show you in which areas your values are strongest.

VALUES SURVEY

Check the column that most closely matches your feelings.

	Very True	Some-times True	Not Sure	Not True
1. I would rather have a large expensive house than own a work of art.				
2. I like to go places with my friends.				
3. I'd really like to travel to far away places.				
4. I think music and art should be required in our schools.				
5. It is important that my family does things together.				
6. I like to make things.				
7. I would rather be president of a club than just a member.				
8. I'd like people to know that I've done something well.				
9. I like to read books that help me understand people.				
10. If I had talent, I'd like to be on TV.				
11. Having an expensive car is something I'd really like.				
12. If I could, I'd like to make a movie that would make people aware of injustice, and would improve the conditions it described.				
13. I'd rather be rich than married.				
14. I like writing stories, plays, or poetry.				
15. I like to try things I've never done before.				
16. I enjoy doing different things.				
17. It is important to be proud of what I do.				
18. If my friends want to do something that I think is wrong, I will not do it.				
19. I'd like to accomplish something in life that will be well known.				
20. A strong family unit is essential to me.				
21. I would disobey a boss who asked me to do something against my principles, even if it meant being fired.				
22. It is important for me to have a good understanding of history.				
23. If I could, I'd like to be president.				
24. It would be fun to climb mountains.				
25. It is very important for me to live in beautiful surroundings.				
26. I like to go to parties.				
27. It is important to have very good friends.				

	Very True	Some-times True	Not Sure	Not True
28. I would rather make gifts than buy them.				
29. I am very close to my mother, father, or both.				
30. I like to attend lectures from which I can learn something.				
31. It is more important to stick to my beliefs than to make money.				
32. I would rather make less money at a job I know would last than take a chance with a job that might not last but pays more.				
33. I would like a lot of expensive possessions.				
34. I would rather be free to move around than be tied down by a family.				
35. I like to feel that I am in charge in a group.				
36. It is important to have an appreciation for art or music.				
37. I like to write.				
38. I'd look forward to taking a job in a city I had never visited before.				
39. Having children is important to me.				
40. I'd like to understand the way a TV works.				
41. I'd like to be able to decide what and how much work I will do during a day.				
42. I'd like to do something that helps people.				
43. I'd like to be famous.				
44. I'd rather be a judge than a lawyer.				
45. I do not think I'd like adventurous vacations.				
46. I would like to have works of art in my home.				
47. I would like a job that gives me plenty of free time to spend with my family.				
48. I could not be happy with a job in which I did not feel good about myself.				
49. I get very nervous when I'm forced to take chances.				
50. I would rather be a boss than a worker.				
51. It is important to share activities with friends.				
52. If I knew how, I would make my own clothes.				
53. I would rather not have to answer to a boss.				

	Very True	Some-times True	Not Sure	Not True
54. Gaining knowledge is important to me.				
55. I'd rather work for a well-established company than a new company that hasn't established itself.				
56. Money can't buy happiness, but it helps.				
57. Being rich would be the best thing about being a movie star.				
58. Being famous would be the best thing about being a movie star.				
59. The best thing about being a movie star is that I'd be doing something creative.				
60. I like to be able to make my own decisions.				
61. Getting to travel would be the best thing about being a movie star.				
62. I'd like to nurse people back to health.				
63. I would like helping tutor people having trouble at school.				
64. I feel more comfortable in places I've seen before than in new places.				
65. I'd like to work at a job in which I help people.				
66. I enjoy spending an evening with my family.				
67. I'd rather work at a job that is not very interesting but pays a lot, than one that is interesting, but pays little.				
68. I would like to write a book that would help people.				
69. I want to be able to travel if the opportunity arises.				
70. If I had the talent, I'd like to be a famous rock star.				
71. I like reading to gain insight into human behavior.				
72. It is important to share your life with someone.				
73. If you don't take chances, you'll never get anywhere, and I like to take chances.				
74. I'd rather be a leader than a follower.				
75. The world would be a terrible place without beautiful things.				
76. It is important to try to learn something new every day.				
77. I would feel I was doing something worthwhile if I helped a friend with her problems.				
78. I especially like things I make myself.				
79. A close family is important to me.				

	Very True	Some-times True	Not Sure	Not True
80. I think it is important to donate to the needy.				
81. I enjoy looking at beautiful scenery.				
82. The best thing about winning a gold medal at the Olympics would be the recognition.				
83. I like to go on hikes (or bike rides) with my friends.				
84. I have strong beliefs about what is right and wrong.				
85. It is important to have a family with whom to discuss problems.				
86. I'd like an exciting life.				
87. I prefer working by myself rather than as part of a team.				
88. I'd like to know all that I can about the workings of nature.				
89. I think it's wrong to help a friend cheat on an exam, even if I know he will fail if I don't help.				
90. Having a job I know I can keep is important to me.				
91. I'd like to have enough money to invest for the future.				
92. I don't like someone assigning me tasks to do.				
93. I do not like being alone very much.				
94. I like to take charge of organizing activities.				
95. I think saving money for the future is very important.				
96. When I've done something I'm proud of, it's important that other people know.				
97. I would rather make less money at a job in which I choose my own work, than make more money at a job in which someone tells me what to do.				
98. People should contribute a small amount of money to be used to decorate public buildings.				
99. I don't like to take risks with money.				
100. I like thinking of something that's never been done before.				
101. I would not like a job in which I traveled a lot and could not have lasting relationships.				
102. If a teacher accidentally left test answers where I could see them, I would not look.				
103. I like people to ask me for my opinion when trying to decide the best way to handle a situation.				
104. If I could, I'd like to make a movie that people would think is beautiful.				

Turn back to the first page of this exercise. Above the words "Very True," write a 9. Above the words "Sometimes True," write a 6. Above the words "Not Sure," write a 3. Above the words "Not True," write a 0. Do the same for each page of the exercise.

Now, for each number listed below, write the numerical value of the response you selected. For example, if on number 1 you selected "Sometimes True," put a 6 on the line next to number 1. When all the lines have been completed, total the numerical responses under each heading.

Family	Adventure	Knowledge	Power
5 _____	3 _____	9 _____	7 _____
20 _____	15 _____	22 _____	23 _____
29 _____	16 _____	30 _____	35 _____
39 _____	24 _____	40 _____	44 _____
47 _____	38 _____	54 _____	50 _____
66 _____	61 _____	71 _____	74 _____
79 _____	73 _____	76 _____	94 _____
85 _____	86 _____	88 _____	103 _____
Total _____	Total _____	Total _____	Total _____

Moral Judgment and Personal Consistency	Money or Wealth	Friendship and Companionship	Recognition
17 _____	1 _____	2 _____	8 _____
18 _____	11 _____	26 _____	10 _____
21 _____	13 _____	27 _____	19 _____
31 _____	33 _____	51 _____	43 _____
48 _____	56 _____	72 _____	58 _____
84 _____	57 _____	83 _____	70 _____
89 _____	67 _____	93 _____	82 _____
102 _____	91 _____	101 _____	96 _____
Total _____	Total _____	Total _____	Total _____

Independence and Freedom	Security	Beauty or Aesthetics	Creativity	Helping Others
34 _____	32 _____	4 _____	6 _____	12 _____
41 _____	45 _____	25 _____	14 _____	42 _____
53 _____	49 _____	36 _____	28 _____	62 _____
60 _____	55 _____	46 _____	37 _____	63 _____
69 _____	64 _____	75 _____	52 _____	65 _____
87 _____	90 _____	81 _____	59 _____	68 _____
92 _____	95 _____	98 _____	78 _____	77 _____
97 _____	99 _____	104 _____	100 _____	80 _____
Total _____	Total _____	Total _____	Total _____	Total _____

97

For which category is your total the highest? That's the value most important to you at present. However, values can change, and in fact, usually do. For this reason, you may wish to take the Values Survey again in a year or two.

What do the categories mean? Descriptions of each category follow.

Family

Someone with a very high score in this category greatly values the closeness of a family. Parents and children feel close to each other and spend much time together. "Family" can also mean other persons or friends who are close to you, if you choose not to join a traditional family. Your inner circle of acquaintances is important. You are a people person. If you score high in this area, you will want a job that allows you plenty of time at home where you can enjoy family and friends. Your work hours should be consistent and stable. You probably would not be happy as a traveling sales representative, a forest ranger, or an international tour guide.

Adventure

In contrast to the preceding, a career that calls for a lot of travel may be just right if you value adventure. You certainly would not be satisfied with a job in which the routine is the same day after day. Your score shows that you would like to have varied job duties and that you are comfortable taking risks.

See how easy this is? But, oops! What if you have high scores in two categories? Could you have a happy family life and lots of adventure, too? It's possible. Here is where you have to make some choices and spend time comparing careers. Which do you value more? If you're an adventure-loving family man, you may have to settle for hang gliding on weekends, or making an expedition through the wilderness each summer, rather than being a foreign correspondent or an international jewel trader.

Knowledge

If you value knowledge, you will want a career that lets you keep on learning. Teaching is an obvious choice, but you might also consider doing research — scientific, historical, political, or whatever. Being a journalist who covers different stories every day and spends time reading reports and interviewing people might also be a good choice.

Power

It's hard to find an entry-level job with a lot of power, but if that's what you value, you'll want to make sure that there's plenty of room for advancement in your chosen field. You should prepare yourself to take a leadership role by pursuing advanced education or by learning more skills in your field. Or, you might want to start your own business. That way you can be president immediately — even if you're the only employee!

Moral Judgment and and Personal Consistency

If you scored high in this category, you'll want to make sure that your career choice is one you feel is worthwhile; that is, one you can be proud of, no matter what other values it mirrors. For example, if you also had a high adventure score, you would probably be more satisfied as a Peace Corps worker than as a bomber pilot.

Money

Obviously, if money is your top value, you will look carefully at potential earnings for any job you take. Since making a lot of money usually entails spending long hours on the job, you should consider your other values in choosing a field which will hold your interest. You may have little time for family, friends, or outside hobbies. Check the salary levels of a wide range of jobs before starting to narrow your choices.

Friendship and Companionship

If friendship and companionship are important to you, your job should involve working closely with others. Being shut away in a laboratory or sitting in a cubicle with an adding machine will probably hold few charms for you. If you get along well with others and can talk easily with people you don't know well, you might consider working in sales or public relations. If having time for close friendships outside of work is important, though, you won't want a job that involves a great deal of travel or overtime.

Recognition

Is recognition what you want? If so, you'll do best choosing something for which you have a talent, something that will let you work to develop the talent. Of course, some fields have more potential for recognition built into them than others. There may be very few world-renowned bus drivers, but the fact remains that in many communities there are bus drivers *everyone* knows and respects. It often depends on how you do your job, not just what job you do.

Aesthetics

People who score high in aesthetics (love of beauty) like to be surrounded by beauty. If this describes you, you might be happy as an interior designer or an art dealer. You might like being a forest ranger at a national park or an executive in a plush office. You would almost certainly be unhappy as a garbage collector or coal miner.

Creativity

Writers and artists are often thought of as creative, but creativity is an important asset in other fields as well. If you value creativity, you will want a career that gives you room to make choices and decisions, to put your ideas into effect and to evaluate the results of your efforts. You probably wouldn't be happy in a job that is rigid or inflexible. You might find a use for your creativity by working as a program director for a senior citizens' group, as an engineer in a large research firm or as a landscape architect.

Helping Others

People who value helping others have traditionally become teachers and nurses. But, there are many other options. Doctors, social workers, psychologists, counselors, writers, politicians, lawyers, dieticians, speech pathologists, and physical therapists are just a few of the career possibilities for those scoring high in this area.

Independence

If you value independence and freedom, you should beware of careers which are rigidly supervised or scheduled. Some sales representative positions allow you a great deal of freedom. People who work on a free-lance basis, or as consultants, may be able to decide where, when and how much work they will do.

Security

Careers with well-established companies, or those in areas that are basic to human needs and not likely to become obsolete, are good choices for someone who values security. Such a person is usually happier with clearly defined work.

Re-examine your values throughout your life to make sure you aren't working hard and giving up things that are important to you for the sake of something you no longer value.

Here's a quick exercise to help demonstrate how each value relates to career choices. Check the choice that would be most reasonable for a person with the value stated in each question.

QUIZ: APPLYING VALUE CATEGORIES

1. A person who greatly values family life would be most happy as
   a. a merchant marine   b. a flight attendant   c. a school counselor

2. An adventurous person might consider a career as
   a. an accountant   b. an overseas diplomat   c. a florist

3. Knowledge and continued learning would be most important in
   a. college teaching   b. working on an assembly line   c. typing

4. A person concerned with power would be best advised to seek a college degree in
   a. philosophy   b. business administration   c. English

5. Moral judgment plays an important part in
   a. cosmetology   b. counseling   c. welding

6. Those most concerned with money might want to be
   a. social workers   b. corporation heads   c. playground supervisors

7. Companionship would be an important part of a job as
   a. a phone installer   b. a tour guide   c. a jewelry repair person

8. Recognition would be most likely gained as
   a. an athlete   b. a plumber   c. a mail deliverer

9. Valuing aesthetics would be especially important for
   a. a truck driver   b. a veterinarian   c. an art critic

10. A person with a need for some creativity might be happiest as
    a. a waiter   b. a cook   c. a cashier

11. Those who want to help others would get the most satisfaction from
    a. film editing   b. scoring music   c. driving an ambulance

12. A person who values independence should investigate a career as
    a. a secretary   b. a free-lance writer   c. an accountant

13. Security would be one advantage to a job as
    a. an assembly line worker   b. a model   c. a manager with a well-established company

101

ANSWERS

1. The answer is *c*. *A school counselor would seldom have to be away from home overnight, and might even have hours like those of his children in school. He might be able to share summer vacations with them, and so forth.*

2. The answer is *b*. *Living in various parts of the world would provide many opportunities for adventure.*

3. The answer here, of course, is *a*. *A college teacher must not only be very knowledgeable, but must keep on learning.*

4. *b* is the correct answer. *This degree would make you eligible for management or executive jobs with the government or with large and powerful corporations.*

5. The correct answer is *b*. *Counselors have a great deal of influence over their clients, and must be careful about any suggestions they make.*

6. The answer is *b*. *American corporation executives are among the most highly paid people in the world.*

7. The correct answer is *b*. *Getting along well with people is essential for the work of tour guide.*

8. The answer is *a*. *It's difficult to gain recognition in a field in which there is little media attention or public interest.*

9. The correct choice is *c*. *An art critic's sensibilities must be very well developed.*

10. The answer is *b*. *With the proper training, cooks or chefs can be extremely creative in their work.*

11. The correct answer is *c*. *Although some solitary professions may also be helpful to others, you probably won't get as much satisfaction from them as you would from working directly with others and seeing the results.*

12. The answer is *b*. *Keep in mind that jobs offering greater independence than others often entail more risk as well.*

13. The answer is *c*. *Jobs that depend heavily on factors that may be beyond your control, such as the economy, or your own youth and beauty, are not good choices for you if you are interested in security.*

Return to the Values Survey and look at the three categories for which your value scores were highest and write them here.

_____

_____

_____

Now think of a career or type of work that combines the three values you listed. As you are thinking, be sure to keep your income requirements from the budget section in mind.

Ginny's Thoughts

Ginny's top three values were power, recognition and helping others. When she thought about jobs that involve power, she came up with a list that included business executive, judge, fashion designer and politician. Ginny knew that there were other jobs that fit, but her list was a start.

Recognition was a trickier area. Realistically, she had to admit that she had no great talent as an athlete, singer or movie star. When she looked back at her "power" list, however, she thought it might be quite possible to make a name for herself in one of those fields.

What about helping others? There were many possibilities, of course. But fields like nursing and social work didn't seem to hold much promise for power and recognition. Looking back at her list, she decided that, while business executives could certainly help society, business was not the right path for her. Fashion designers could be said to be helpful to others, but that really wasn't what she had in mind. Now, judges and politicians . . . "Hmm," she thought, "maybe I should think about going to law school, the place to start for either of those professions."

What about you? Can you come up with some careers that have elements of each of the top three values?

How do your present values relate to careers you might choose? Quickly think of jobs which encompass your values. Get your family or friends to help, and complete the sentences below.

I should look into finding out more about becoming a _____

_____

because I value _____

_____

_____

_____

and this career would allow me to _____

_____

_____

_____

I should look into finding out more about becoming a _____

_____

because I value _____

_____

_____

_____

and this career would allow me to _____

_____

_____

_____

Did you come up with any new careers you'd like to investigate further?

_____

Now that you have looked at the activities you like, and more generally, at the things you value, reflect on your conclusions and write a statement about them.

What is Most Important to Me?

_____

_____

_____

_____

_____

_____

_____

_____

_____

_____

_____

_____

_____

_____

_____

_____

_____

_____

Date _____

Goal Setting

Have you ever stopped to wonder what makes some people successful? Talents and abilities are certainly important, but an equally important aspect of success is knowing what you want. When you do, you can consciously choose actions that will lead toward your goal.

Major businesses define what they want and where they are going by setting goals, and then listing ways to achieve those goals. Their plans for meeting the goal are called objectives. Objectives, in other words, are the measurable steps you will take to reach your goal. Successful people often use the same approach to help them plan their actions.

Lynn's Story

Lynn wanted to lose 15 pounds right before her school reunion. She followed a diet with menus of under 1,000 calories a day, and started a daily exercise program. She weighed herself each morning and kept a progress chart inside her closet door— right next to her graduation picture. She allowed herself a reasonable amount of time to lose weight. She charted her progress, kept her goal in mind, and she met it!

Lynn looked terrific at the reunion, and her success gave her a sense of confidence she hadn't known before. She began to think about her former classmates and some of the interesting careers they had taken up. Lynn had been bored with her old job for years, but didn't think she could change professions at this stage of her life. She changed her mind and set a new goal—to be admitted to a Master's degree program by the following autumn.

By looking back at Lynn's story, you can see the importance of having a goal. Goals identify a desired behavior or achievement to be completed within a set amount of time. After a goal is set, it really helps if you can measure progress toward it. Lynn's first goal could be measured by weighing herself on the day of the reunion — either she had lost the 15 pounds or she hadn't. If she is admitted to graduate school next year, she will have reached her second goal.

Goals need to be measured so that you can clearly determine whether or not you have acheived them. Setting a completion date or deadline not only tells you whether or not you have been successful, but helps you set up plans for specific actions.

While Lynn was dieting, her first objective was to limit her daily food intake to 1,000 calories. The second was to carry out ten exercises on a daily schedule. She did a bit of research and learned that if she followed this schedule she could be assured a reasonable chance of success. If she is also going to go back to school, she will have to set objectives concerning which programs to apply for, and when.

The more specific you can be in stating a goal and your steps for reaching it, the better your chance for success. General goals such as, "I want to be happy," or "I want to be a success," need to be broken down into smaller, more immediately attainable parts. What would make you happy? Would you consider yourself successful if you were rich? How much money would you need to feel you were rich?

An example of a more specific goal would be, "to make $50,000 a year within ten years."

With this goal, objectives could be:

1. By next week, research ten careers that pay $50,000 a year.
2. Take a vocational interest survey within the month.
3. Within 2 months, apply to four colleges or training schools that prepare for possible career choices.
4. By next year, sign up for classes that will meet college requirements.

Another example of a specific goal could be "to be married to the same person for the rest of my life."

Objectives for this goal could be:

1. By next month, list my values and those I would like my partner to share.
2. Spend one day a week in activities in which I would be likely to meet someone who shares my interests: church, hikes, folk dancing, and music programs, for example.
3. Once married, set aside at least one hour a day for total attention to my partner.

The second example we've described illustrates that with any goal you choose, there's no guarantee that you will be successful. No one can say with certainty that you will marry and stay married for 25 years. However, there are many things you can do to improve your chances for success. You can make sure you understand yourself and that you take part in activities that will increase your chances of meeting someone with whom you are compatible. Later, you can engage in activities that will help enrich and maintain your marriage.

Set Your Own Goals

Direct practice is the most effective method for learning to set and use goals and objectives.

Write two goals that you would like to achieve for each time period listed here. As you write, consider whether or not the goal can be measured. That is, will you be able to tell without a doubt if your goal has been reached?

Today's Goals

EXAMPLE: Read two articles on self-improvement.

1. _____

_____

2. _____

_____

3. _____

_____

4. _____

_____

This Week's Goals

EXAMPLE: Run a total of 20 miles.

1. _____
   _____

2. _____
   _____

3. _____
   _____

4. _____
   _____

This Year's Goals

EXAMPLE: Write for catalogues of five colleges or trade schools I might
           want to attend.

1. _____
   _____

2. _____
   _____

3. _____
   _____

4. _____
   _____

"Within the Next Five Years" Goals

EXAMPLE: Earn a Master's Degree in Business Administration.

1. _____
   _____

2. _____
   _____

3. _____
   _____

4. _____
   _____

Objectives

The Action Plan

1. What will be different?
2. By how many, or how much?
3. By when?

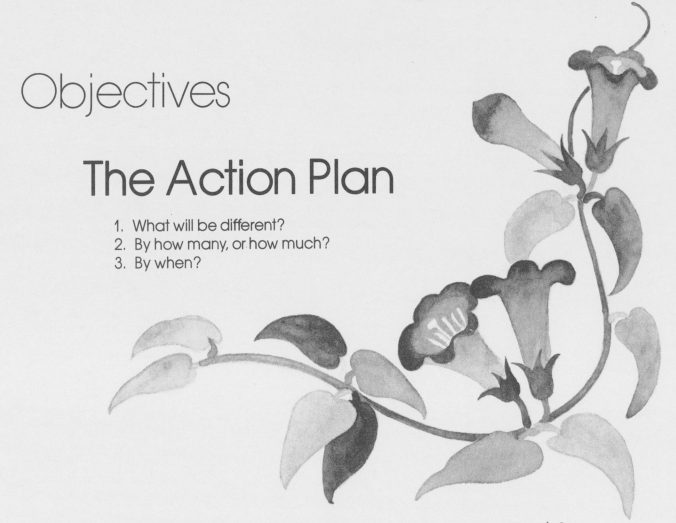

Setting goals is one thing. Reaching your goals will require specific actions on your part. But why? How do you know what your objectives should be? It sometimes takes research to come up with a sound action plan.

If your goals are very specific, objectives will often suggest themselves. If you want to lose 15 pounds in ten weeks, you will need to lose a pound and a half each week. By research you will find that you need to limit your eating to 1,200 calories a day. When objectives are less obvious, it may help to ask yourself these questions: What will be different when I have reached my goal? By how many, or how much? By when?

Diagramming your objectives can be a big help. Once you learn how, you'll find that stating them becomes almost automatic. Here's how to diagram. Begin by asking yourself, "What will be different?" Underline it. Then ask, "By how many?" Use a triangle, like the one in the example that follows, to show this step. "By when?" Draw a circle around the date.

EXAMPLE
If your goal is to make your own holiday gifts, an objective might be to knit three pair of mittens by December 15. A diagram of this objective would look like this:

To knit three pair of mittens by December 15.

For practice, diagram the objectives for the goals that follow.

EXERCISE 1: Diagramming Goals and Objectives

Goal: To learn word processing on the computer within three months.

Objective: To investigate three training programs by next week.

To practice one hour a day, six days per week, until competent.

Goal: To go on vacation to Hawaii next year.

Objective: To save $50 a month for the next 10 months.

To watch the paper every day for a charter special.

Goal: To increase my endurance and physical strength for my fire fighter vocational exam next month.

Objective: To do 30 minutes of physical exercise each morning.

To take a brisk 2 mile walk each evening.

Goal: To complete my requirements for professional licensing by next year.

Objective: To study my assignments for at least one hour a day.

To read one professional book or journal each week.

Now write and diagram *two objectives* for each of the following goals. Make sure that each of your objectives includes all three of the diagram components.

Goal: To get a job that meets my financial goals by next year.

Objective: _____

Objective: _____

Goal: To increase my typing (keyboarding) speed by 20 words per minute.

Objective: _____

Objective: _____

Goal: To save enough money to visit my family next year.

Objective: _____

Objective: _____

What goals have you set for yourself? To get practice setting objectives, write one goal that you hope to achieve in your career, one goal involving your friends or relatives, and one goal for your future. Set two objectives for each goal and diagram them to show what will be different, by how much, and by when.

EXERCISE 2: Writing Goals and Objectives

1. Write one goal with two objectives that involves career training or career advancement.

Goal: _____

_____

Objective: _____

_____

Objective: _____

_____

2. Write one goal with two objectives that involves friends or relatives.

Goal: _____

_____

Objective: _____

_____

Objective: _____

_____

3. Write one goal with two objectives that relates to your future.

Goal: _____

_____

Objective: _____

_____

Objective: _____

_____

4. Write one goal and two objectives that relate to your achieving a behavior you consider desirable for yourself. Turn back to page 31 and review the desired behavior change.

Goal: _____

_____

Objective: _____

_____

Objective: _____

_____

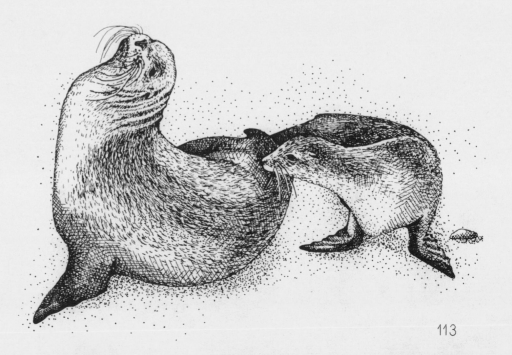

REFLECTIONS

CHAPTER FIVE

How Do You Get There From Here?

Decision making

On this narrow planet, we have
only the choice between two
unknown worlds.
— Colette
    French writer

No trumpets sound when
the important decisions of our
life are made. Destiny is made
known silently.
— Agnes De Mille
    Choreographer

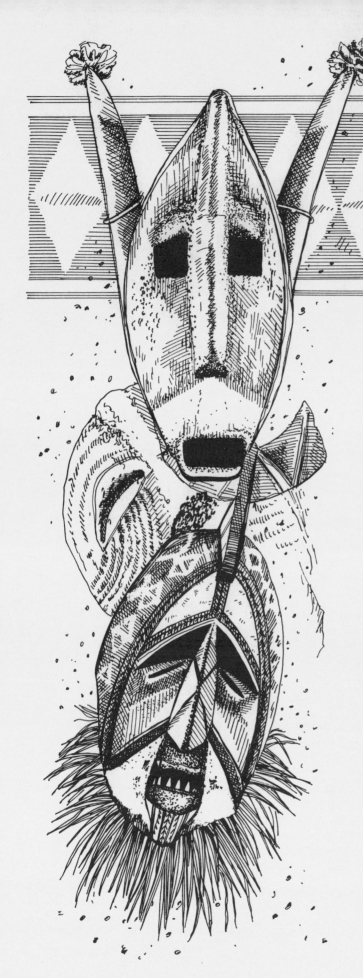

If you've ever felt controlled by events or by others, you know how upsetting it can be. One of life's worst frustrations is feeling that you have no control over your own actions. In contrast, there are few greater satisfactions than choosing your own direction in life and making things go your own way. How do people gain such control? Most have learned to consciously make decisions that reflect their *values* and *goals*.

Keeping your values and goals in mind when you make decisions is not as hard as it might sound. In fact, you probably already do it in many situations. Remember that sweater your great Aunt Lucy — the one who lives across the country — sent you? The one with all those garish sequins that made you look like a fish with shimmering scales? Because you *valued* her thoughtfulness, you promptly sent a thank you note. And, because your *goal* is to be a person with taste and consideration for others, you quickly made the *decision* to contribute the sweater to the charity rummage sale. (When you see your neighbor wearing it at the supermarket several weeks later, of course you smile and agree that, yes, someone certainly was foolish to give up such a treasure.)

Choosing a proper course of action is often more difficult than it was with Aunt Lucy's sweater. What are the steps to making better decisions when things are less clear cut? In this chapter you will learn a logical step-by-step way to keep your values and goals in focus. You should find it helpful in almost any situation.

Sandy's Story

When my first child, Rick, was born twelve years ago, I quit my job as a teacher to be at home with him. Then Ryan came along two years later, and my husband, Larry, and I decided it was important for me to continue to be a full-time mom. Now, though, Rick and Ryan have school and so many outside activities that they don't really need me at home. I've been thinking of going back to school to prepare for a new career. Teaching doesn't appeal to me the way it used to.

Larry thinks it makes more sense to use the skills I already have. Why spend all that time and money on education at my age, he says, when I could get a good job without it. The boys aren't exactly enthusiastic about the idea, either. They think I should be available to drive them to their activities after school, and that a new job would take up too much of my time. They think teaching is the best thing for me to do, too.

My parents, on the other hand, want me to stay at home. My mom never worked while I was growing up, and they don't think I should, either. The women in my bridge club agree with my parents. They seem happy with their situation, and that's fine, but I really want to do some kind of outside work, and they don't seem to understand why I feel this way.

Should I go back to school? Should I get a teaching job? Or should I just forget the whole idea? It's all so difficult and confusing. How can I make the best decision for my family—and for me?

Have you ever felt like Sandy? Have you ever felt as if the world was spinning away from you and you didn't know what to do? Sometimes the constant decisions of daily living make people feel that way. Think about a typical day for a woman, you, if you like. Write down ten decisions a woman might make during a typical day.

1. _____

2. _____

3. _____

4. _____

5. _____

6. _____

7. _____

8. _____

9. _____

10. _____

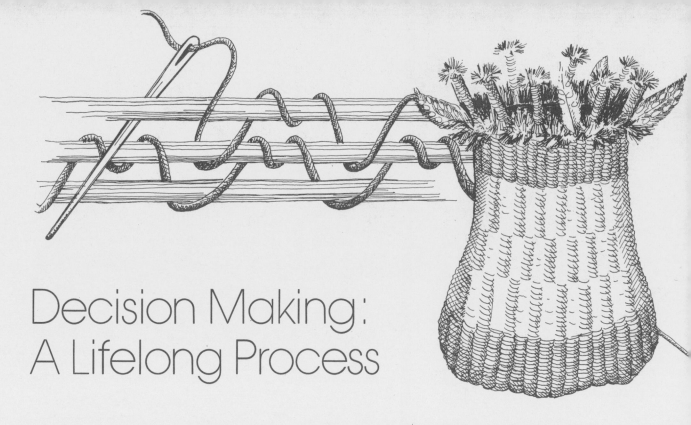

Decision Making:
A Lifelong Process

Making decisions starts in infancy and continues throughout our lives. The kinds of decisions we make change as our lives progress. For comparison, list some decisions a person might make at the ages given here.

5 years old _____

_____

15 years old _____

_____

20 years old _____

_____

40 years old _____

_____

Whether you realize it or not, decisions you made in your teens affect the way you live now. You decided about your future training and education and how you would cope with social issues and friendships. You had to deal with love, and, quite possibly, drugs or alcohol.

Pressure from others makes decision making more difficult. The following responses are often heard when women attempt to make decisions for their own futures.

"What about the children?"
"Your first responsibility is to your family."
"A woman's place is in the home."

As you make your decisions, you may be tempted to give in to these outside pressures. Or you may try to put off making the decision altogether. When this temptation arises, remind yourself that, however you do it, decision making can't be avoided.

Not Deciding is Making a Decision

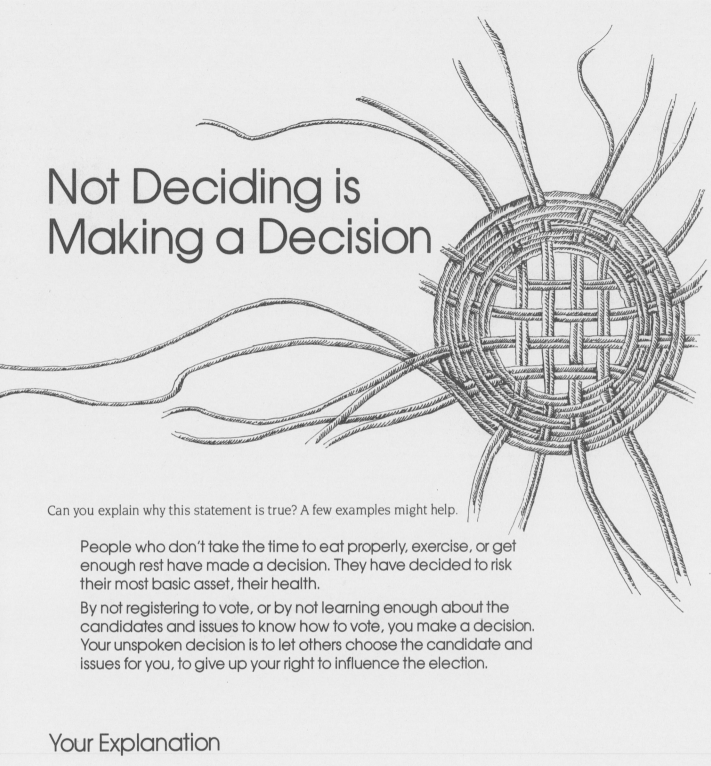

Can you explain why this statement is true? A few examples might help.

People who don't take the time to eat properly, exercise, or get enough rest have made a decision. They have decided to risk their most basic asset, their health.

By not registering to vote, or by not learning enough about the candidates and issues to know how to vote, you make a decision. Your unspoken decision is to let others choose the candidate and issues for you, to give up your right to influence the election.

Your Explanation

_____

_____

_____

_____

_____

Decisions are made in hopes of bringing about a desired goal. The following four-step procedure will assist you in making decisions that will help you achieve your goal.

Decision-Making Process

STEP 1: State the decision to be made or the problem to be solved.

The first step is to state the decision to be made or the problem to be solved. In Sandy's case, for example, the decision to be made is to choose her future career.

Whenever a decision involves planning for the future, it is helpful to examine the decision in terms of stated goals.

The decision or problem: What life course should Sandy follow?

Sandy's goals: To have a job she finds satisfying.
To be economically self-sufficient.

Sandy can now begin to approach decision making in terms of achieving her goals. Note that her stated goals are not the only possibilities. She also has the following options:

1. To have a job that pays $40,000 a year.
2. To have a job that lets her be home when her children are.
3. To enter the workforce immediately.
4. To have a job she can do in her own home.

Before making her decision, Sandy decides to examine her options more closely. She hasn't worked as a teacher for a dozen years, so she does some research to find out if things have changed. She also takes an interest inventory to find out what kinds of jobs she is likely to find satisfying, and sends for catalogues from colleges within commuting distance of her home. An interview with a counselor at the college she finds most interesting tells her even more.

As she goes through the decision-making process, Sandy keeps her options open. This is important, because it provides many more choices later. Like many decisions a person makes in life, Sandy's will not be irreversible. If she decides to go back to school, and then doesn't like it, she can still decide to be a teacher, or to return to her life as a homemaker. But if she *does* get another college degree, she will have more choices in the kind of job she has, and she might have additional money to make financial choices, too.

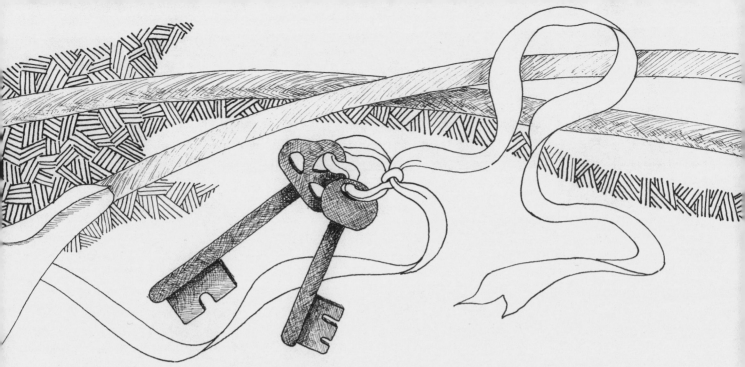

Every decision has an effect on the person who makes it but the choices are not necessarily right or wrong. Once Sandy realized that her first goal was to have a job she found satisfying, choices became clearer. Choosing whether to go back to school or back to teaching then became the biggest problem. Her family wanted her to teach, but she was interested in taking on a challenge. She loved her family, but she had a duty to herself, too.

Sandy stated her goal as "Choose the job I will find most satisfying." In the spaces provided, list other goals she could have chosen.

1. _____

_____

_____

2. _____

_____

_____

3. _____

_____

_____

4. _____

_____

_____

5. _____

_____

_____

STEP 2: Find and List Alternatives

The next step toward achieving a goal or solving a problem is to list alternatives. Sandy's alternatives are to go back to school, to go back to teaching, or to stay home with her family. Just listing choices, in this instance, does not help her decide. Often an acceptable choice will present itself if you simply list alternatives.

The next step is to examine the advantages and disadvantages of each alternative. Here's Sandy's comparison:

Alternative	Advantages	Disadvantages
Going back to school	More satisfying future Possibility for higher-paying job Opportunity for growth	Time away from family with no economic pay-off Career change equals lifestyle change
Going back to teaching	Immediate economic pay-off More time with family due to schedule	Low job satisfaction Little chance for advancement
Staying home with her family	More time for relationships More time for herself	No economic security Doesn't meet her need to be intellectually challenged

If you were in Sandy's position, which would you choose? _____

Why? _____

_____

_____

Sandy makes a decision, not to stay home. She is confident she will be able to meet her family's needs and a change is really what she wants.

To choose between the remaining possibilities, Sandy must consider her own needs. Does she value a new career enough to make the commitment to go back to school? Only Sandy can answer that question.

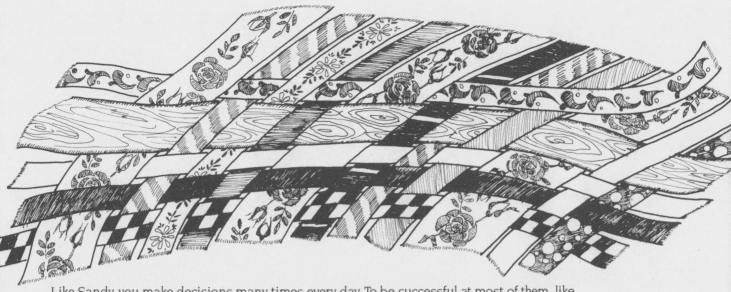

Like Sandy, you make decisions many times every day. To be successful at most of them, like deciding what to wear, what to eat, who to spend time with, or where to go in your free time, doesn't require stating your goals. Yet goals are involved just the same. To see what we mean, list four things you consider when you make the decisions listed here.

A. Deciding what to wear:

    1. _____

    2. _____

    3. _____

    4. _____

B. Deciding what to eat:

    1. _____

    2. _____

    3. _____

    4. _____

C. Deciding who to spend time with:

    1. _____

    2. _____

    3. _____

    4. _____

D. Deciding where to go in your free time:

    1. _____

    2. _____

    3. _____

    4. _____

Now state one goal for each decision in the preceding list.

1. _____

2. _____

3. _____

4. _____

Whether or not your decisions are what most people would consider major ones, such as the choice of a career, or marriage partner, clarifying your thought processes by stating goals can be very helpful. Almost everything you do requires some decisions.

Lucinda's Story

Lucinda, for example, had been working at her current job for a year, and she thought she deserved a raise. Although Lucinda's supervisor had praised her, she never said anything about an increase in pay. Lucinda enjoyed her work, but she became angry every time she saw the all too familiar amount on her paycheck. What could Lucinda do to get the raise she thinks she deserves?

Lucinda's goal is to get a raise in pay. Here's her analysis of that goal.

Alternatives	Advantages	Disadvantages
Ask supervisor for raise	Will know for sure if supervisor values my work Get the raise	Supervisor may say "no" Takes courage Supervisor may be resentful
Work harder and hope someone notices	No risk involved Builds character	Time consuming Results not guaranteed Someone may not notice
Quit and look for new job	Get out of uncomfortable situation Find a better job	No job, no money May not find a job as good as this one

What Can You Do?

For this exercise we'd like you to list alternatives for each of the following situations, using Lucinda's model as an example.

DECISION 1

Tracy has been married to Dave for two years. They don't have any children. Usually Dave is a good partner, but sometimes he drinks too much and becomes abusive to Tracy. At first, he just yelled a lot. Now, though, he hits her sometimes. Last night he gave her a black eye and badly bruised her arm. The situation is clearly getting worse. What can Tracy do?

What is the decision to be made? _____

_____

_____

_____

Goal? _____

_____

_____

_____

Now list your alternatives and their pros and cons.

Alternative Decisions	Advantages	Disadvantages
1.		
2.		
3.		

DECISION 2

You have been married for ten years and have three children, ages two, four, and six. You finished high school and worked for awhile as a telephone operator before your children were born. Your husband decides that he wants a divorce. You are forced to sell your house so you and your husband can divide your possessions equally. The amount of money you receive from your former husband is not enough to live on. What can you do?

What is the decision to be made? _____

_____

_____

_____

Goal? _____

_____

Alternative Decisions	Advantages	Disadvantages
1.		
2.		
3.		

DECISION 3

Your husband is a college dean and you are a professor of astronomy. You have been offered an important position at a university in another state. The position is at a much higher salary, and it would allow you to do work you've always wanted to do. You have two children ages 12 and 14. You know you will probably not get another chance like this. Your husband would have to take a lower-paying job if he were to move with you. What can you do?

What is the decision to be made? _____

_____

_____

_____

Goal? _____
_____
_____
_____

Alternative Decisions	Advantages	Disadvantages
1. _____		
2. _____		
3. _____		

DECISION 4

You are fifty-five years old, and have been working as a registered nurse for thirty years. You are a widow and your children are grown and on their own. You would like to do something different with your life, and are thinking about joining the Peace Corps or Vista. It would mean giving up your secure job, making a complete change in your lifestyle, and you wonder if you are too old. But you can't seem to stop thinking about the rewarding work, the challenge and the excitement. What should you do?

What is the decision to be made? _____
_____
_____

Goal? _____
_____
_____
_____

Alternative Decisions	Advantages	Disadvantages
1. _____		
2. _____		
3. _____		

127

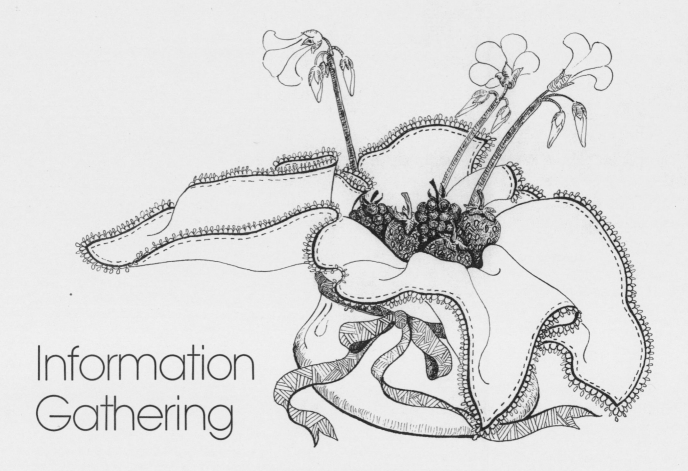

Information Gathering

Have you ever heard anyone use the term "informed decision"? It usually refers to a decision based on facts and thought, a logical decision, or perhaps the best possible decision under a particular set of circumstances.

To make an informed decision you need information — as much of it as you can get. The more information you have about a problem, the more alternatives you'll have in making a decision. That way, you're more likely to make the best decision.

The number of alternatives you were able to list for the situations in the last exercise depended mainly on the information you were given. That is why it is sometimes said that information is power. Gathering information is one of the most crucial aspects of decision-making.

Before gathering information, you have to determine what you need to know. For example, Meredith and Sam would like to get married. Both have been married before, and each has two children. The children are opposed to the marriage. Sam and Meredith can't decide whose house they would live in. Their children go to different schools.

What information do Sam and Meredith need before making their decision? _____

_____

_____

_____

_____

_____

The decision Sam and Meredith will be making is personal, yet it will probably be influenced by others. Their relatives, children and friends, for instance, will no doubt exert strong pressures.

List some objections they might hear from relatives, children and friends who oppose the marriage.

_____

_____

_____

_____

List some statements they might hear in favor of the marriage.

_____

_____

_____

_____

The purpose of examining pressures is to emphasize that decisions are not made in a social vacuum. Being aware of pressure helps keep it under control. This awareness is extremely important in the next step of the decision-making process. Let us look at that step right now.

STEP 3: Evaluating Alternatives

In Step 1 you stated the decision you needed to make, or the problem you needed to solve. Then, in Step 2, you found and listed your alternatives. Step 3 in the decision-making process involves examining your alternatives. You need to find out as much about each one as you reasonably can. To gather helpful information you can read, talk to people, make observations, watch television, or do whatever is necessary. In evaluating information, always ask yourself:

1. On what basis does this person claim to know something about this topic I'm interested in?
2. Does he or she have any ulterior reason for telling me this?

In this state of decision making, it is helpful to list how much you know about each alternative and the advantages or disadvantages of each.

For example, suppose you are thinking about whether or not you want a job. Your alternatives are:

1. To get a job.
2. Not to get a job.
3. Start a business.

Evaluating each alternative, you could state advantages and disadvantages like those shown here.

Alternatives	Advantages	Disadvantages
Get a job	Money Experience	Less free time Less time for family Less time for self
No job	More free time More time for family More time for personal pursuits	No money No experience
Start a business	Money Experience Independence	Same as get a job

To make your decision, in light of the advantages and disadvantages of your alternatives, you need to consider:

1. The amount of free time you need.
2. How important full-time attention to the family is.
3. Whether or not you really need the money.
4. Whether the experience gained is likely to be helpful to you.

Listing alternatives and carefully evaluating the choices provides a framework for clear and logical thinking. Let's examine the process in working through another sample decision.

Maritza's Story

Maritza enjoyed her role as full-time wife and mother, but now the children have grown up and moved away. She has always dreamed of going to college, and she thinks that this is the ideal time to stop dreaming and start making plans. She was a good student in high school, but her family likes to remind her that was a long time ago. The community college offers a special program for older students, with classes to help brush up rusty study skills. Maritza took the college entrance exams last year, though, and did well enough to be admitted to the local university. A friend suggested that Maritza should start out just taking some evening courses, to see if she likes being a student. Maritza's fantasy of college life, however, involves strolling through the campus on bright autumn days, having philosophical discussions with other students over coffee in the union, and spending long afternoons doing research in the library. Sometimes she worries that she is overconfident, and that she really wouldn't be able to do college-level work, after all.

Maritza's goal: To attend college.

What are her alternatives? _____
_____
_____

What does she need to know to evaluate her alternatives? _____
_____
_____

List the advantages and disadvantages of each alternative that can be determined from what you know about the situation.

Alternatives	Advantages	Disadvantages

STEP 4: Considering the Odds

Once you've listed alternatives and gathered and examined the information available to you, you are in the best position to know the *probable* outcome of any decision. It's rarely certain that a particular decision will lead to a desired outcome, but an informed decision can significantly improve the chances of things working out in your favor. Had Wanda used the decision-making steps, she might have saved herself some pain. Her story follows.

Wanda's Story

Wanda went on a skiing trip with friends. She was a beginning skier and all her friends were better than she. Wanda knew she should take lessons but lessons were expensive. Her friends told her all she needed was a little practice and asked her to go with them to the more difficult ski runs.

Wanda's alternatives were:

1. Take lessons
2. Ski by herself on the easy slopes
3. Go with her friends

She decided to ski with her friends and ended up with a badly broken leg. She said later, "I just wanted to be with them, and not have to admit I couldn't ski as well as they could."

Looking back and examining the possible outcomes of each alternative, we see that she could have done the following:

Alternative	Probable Outcomes
Taken lessons	Learned to ski better Had less money for other things
Skied alone	Been lonely Not as much fun Improved through practice
Skied with friends	Had a great time Improved through practice Could get hurt

These were the possible results of each choice. To determine how probable they might be (to consider the odds), Wanda needed to be realistic about her skiing ability, and how difficult the slopes were. What information could she use to make these judgments?

Let's review the decision-making steps. They'll be a valuable aid to you throughout your life, whatever the decisions you need to make.

1. State the goal to be achieved or the problem to be solved.
2. List alternatives.
3. Evaluate the alternatives.
4. Consider the odds or probable outcomes.

The four steps appear simple, yet you undoubtedly know from your own experiences that making a decision is often difficult. Decisions are difficult because each of us is a complex individual with unique needs, values, and her own personality. This is why we need to learn how to gather and evaluate information.

It's time to practice making a real-life decision for yourself. In the space below, use the four-step process to make a decision about a goal you want to reach or a problem you need to solve within the next three months.

1. Decision to be made: _____

_____

Alternatives	Advantages	Disadvantages	Probable Outcome
1.			
2.			
3.			
4.			

Strategies — Decision-Making Patterns

There are many decision-making patterns. We'll list some in a moment that you might recognize in your own behavior. Most don't work as well as the four-step process you just learned. In fact, sometimes they can lead to disastrous results. Most of us have a tendency to use one or more of these patterns from time to time. Do you? Some of the patterns most often used are described below. See if you can think of other examples for each. Take them from your own experience, examples in this book, or any other source you'd like.

WISH PATTERN

Definition: Choosing an alternative that could lead to the most desirable result, regardless of risk.

EXAMPLE: You choose someone to marry hoping to change his bad habits.

_____

_____

_____

ESCAPE PATTERN

Definition: Choosing an alternative in order to avoid the worst possible result.

EXAMPLE: You stay at a job that makes you unhappy because you are afraid you'll dislike a new one even more.

_____

_____

_____

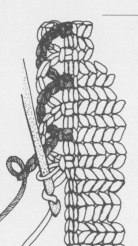

SAFE PATTERN

Definition: Choosing the alternative that is most likely to bring success.

EXAMPLE: You take an art class knowing you are a good artist, rather than taking another course in which you do not know how well you will do.

_____

_____

_____

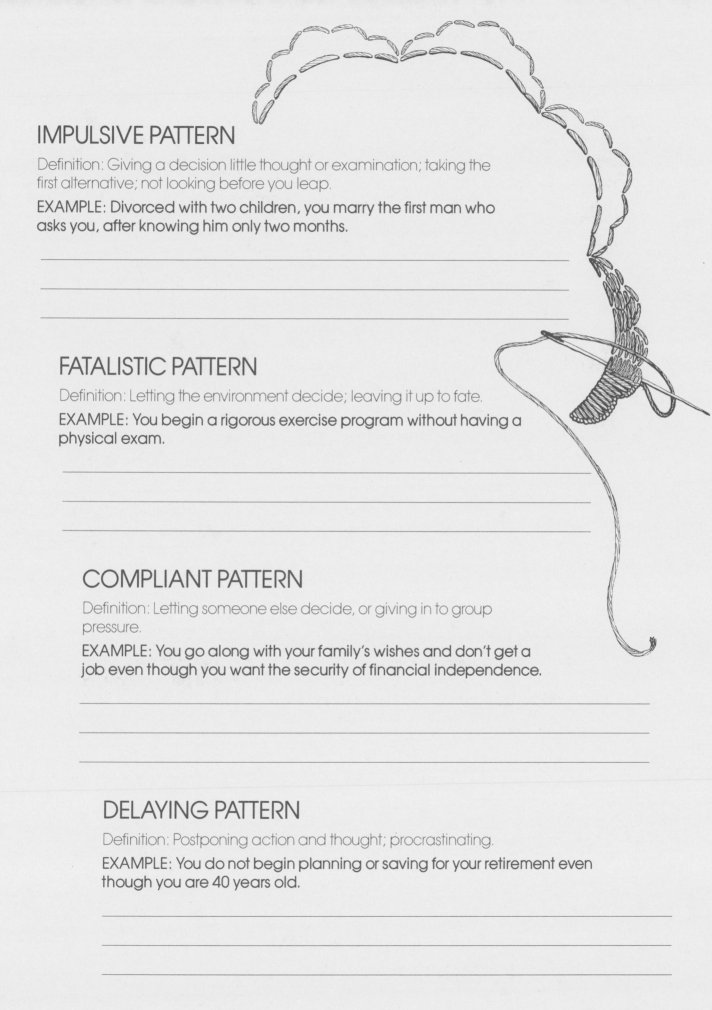

IMPULSIVE PATTERN

Definition: Giving a decision little thought or examination; taking the first alternative; not looking before you leap.

EXAMPLE: Divorced with two children, you marry the first man who asks you, after knowing him only two months.

_____

_____

_____

FATALISTIC PATTERN

Definition: Letting the environment decide; leaving it up to fate.

EXAMPLE: You begin a rigorous exercise program without having a physical exam.

_____

_____

_____

COMPLIANT PATTERN

Definition: Letting someone else decide, or giving in to group pressure.

EXAMPLE: You go along with your family's wishes and don't get a job even though you want the security of financial independence.

_____

_____

_____

DELAYING PATTERN

Definition: Postponing action and thought; procrastinating.

EXAMPLE: You do not begin planning or saving for your retirement even though you are 40 years old.

_____

_____

_____

AGONIZING PATTERN

Definition: Getting so overwhelmed by alternatives that you don't know what to do.

EXAMPLE: The kids are grown, you are talented, bright and skilled and have many job offers that would increase your status and earning power. You can't make up your mind which one to take, or even whether you should accept a job at all.

_____

_____

_____

PLANNING PATTERN

Definition: Using a procedure so that the end result is satisfying; a rational approach.

EXAMPLE: You decide to take a job with a company with much potential for advancement.

_____

_____

_____

INTUITIVE PATTERN

Definition: Making a choice on the basis of vague feelings, or because "it feels right."

EXAMPLE: You choose a job because you like the design of the company's office. You don't talk to the person who will be your boss, or find out about the benefits package.

_____

_____

_____

Which pattern do you think you use the most?

_____

_____

_____

_____

Risk Taking

Making decisions involves taking a certain amount of risk. But then, so does *not* making a decision. There's no getting around it. Women are often called poor risk takers because they have, in the past, had a tendency to do what was safe and easy (in other words, what men and tradition said they should do). Actually, millions of women take *huge* risks every day. What, for example, could be more risky than not being able to support yourself?

It's impossible to say that risk taking, as such, is good or bad. While taking some kinds of risks is dangerous and foolish, taking others can lead to a more exciting and satisfying life. Those are the kinds of risks you want to take — the ones that can help you achieve a goal or solve a problem, without courting disaster.

Strangely enough, it may be easier to take immense risks with your financial survival than to do something you've always wanted to do. Many people are afraid to attempt new things because they fear they will fail or look silly. Women, especially, have been brought up to "play it safe." The typical little boy may learn on the baseball field that losing is not the end of the world — there's always tomorrow. At the same time his sister may be receiving a lecture from Mom on why she shouldn't ride her bicycle in gravel; after all, she might fall and get hurt.

Such attitudes can hurt you when you start planning for a career or when you begin working. Of course you may not always get into programs you want, or maybe you won't get raises or promotions when you expect them. But that doesn't mean you shouldn't try. If you "play it safe" you have nothing to lose, but nothing to gain either. If you make an effort, you will at least be able to respect yourself for trying.

137

Elaine's Story

Elaine, for example, always dreamed of running for a political office. She didn't need to be President of the United States (at least not right away), but she thought it would be exciting to be in city government. She began working as a political volunteer when she was fourteen, graduted from law school at twenty-four, and went to work for the city attorney's office. When Elaine was thirty-five, she was asked to consider running for mayor. At first Elaine was elated, but soon she began to panic. What if she lost? What if she made a fool of herself?

When she thought the matter through calmly, Elaine realized that there was no way she could be elected if she didn't run. She would have to either give up her dream without even trying, or she would have to take a chance and run for mayor. She decided to run. The worst that could happen, after all, was that she would lose the election. She decided her dream was worth the risk of a little embarrassment.

Elaine took the risk and won the election. She went on to be elected to the state Senate. Some people think she will be the next governor of her state.

Elaine's risk wasn't a large one, yet it led to big changes in her life. Like Elaine, you will have to take some chances in order to achieve your goals. But, usually, you can break your goal into smaller, more easily managed steps that will lessen the risks involved. Taking small risks is good practice, because it will help you manage the bigger ones when they present themselves.

You can use the four-step decision-making process we have discussed to judge whether a risk is worth taking. The steps can also help you find better ways to reach your goal or solve a problem. Here are the steps again:

1. State your goal or problem
2. List your alternatives
3. Evaluate
4. Consider the odds

While we're talking about risks, it's worth noting that some risks are never worth taking. These include smoking, driving when you've been drinking, risking your health, not paying your taxes and hoping someone won't notice, not maintaining your car, leaving your house unlocked, and not preparing for your future.

Do you currently have a goal or problem which might involve some kind of risk? Are you agonizing over something that involves effort but might not be rewarded? Do you have to make a decision where there's a chance you'll lose something? Do you have to make a decision in an area in which you have limited experience? If so, use the four-step process to help you decide if you should take the risk, or, if there's a better way to get the results you want.

1. Goal to be reached or problem to be solved

_____

_____

Alternatives	Advantages	Disadvantages	Probable Outcome
1.			
2.			
3.			
4.			

REFLECTIONS

Courage is the price life exacts
for granting peace.
— Amelia Earhart
  Aviator

CHAPTER SIX

Getting What You Want

Assertiveness

Assertiveness — Taking Charge of Your Life

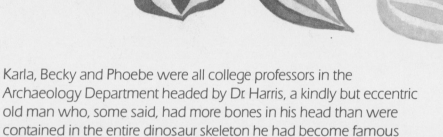

Karla, Becky and Phoebe were all college professors in the Archaeology Department headed by Dr. Harris, a kindly but eccentric old man who, some said, had more bones in his head than were contained in the entire dinosaur skeleton he had become famous for unearthing.

One day, after sitting in on Karla's lecture, Dr. Harris had a suggestion: "Wouldn't it be interesting," he said, "if you delivered your lecture in Greek? Balancing an urn on your head?"

"You old geek," Karla replied. "Wouldn't it be interesting if you finally retired and let someone with an unpetrified brain take over the department?"

Dr. Harris was still alert enough to recognize impertinence when he heard it, and Karla soon found herself out of a job.

Shortly after that incident, Dr. Harris met Becky in the hall outside his office. "Won't you come in?" he asked. "I just finished cataloging 879 different kinds of dirt, and if you have six or eight hours to spare, I'd be happy to show them to you."

"You're kind to offer," Becky said. "But I have a class starting in exactly two minutes, and committee meetings for the rest of the day. Work before pleasure, you know."

"Of course you do. How silly of me to forget. You go on about your business."

As Becky scampered away and Dr. Harris turned to go back in to his office, he saw Phoebe come around the corner, and offered to show her his magnificent collection of dirt.

"Sure," Phoebe told him. "I can't think of anything I'd rather do." Phoebe was actually supposed to be preparing for a lecture, she had appointments with three students, and an important paper to prepare for the archaeology conference in Las Vegas, but what could she do? It's not polite to say no, is it?

How would you handle unwanted attention or advice? For years it was considered "feminine" to be like Phoebe — to give in, to lie, rather than say what you really thought and felt. True, saying "yes" to everyone may make some people like you for awhile. Eventually there comes the day when you accept three appointments for the same night, and you end up scheming, lying, and making people angry. Worst of all, *other* people seem to control your life, not you.

When they realize what is happening, many women, like Phoebe, become so angry that they lose all regard for other people's feelings, as Karla did. Becoming furious is understandable when it seems that everyone is trying to manipulate you, or that everyone is making unfair demands. Being harsh and tactless definitely lets others know what you think. But they probably won't like you or want to honor your feelings.

As is so often the case, the middle ground is the best route to take. You can be in control of your life, and still be liked and respected. The way to do it is by engaging in assertive behavior. That is, by expressing yourself honestly, but with tact and respect for the feelings of others.

You've already come a long way on the road to taking charge of your life. You've looked at who you are and how you got that way. You know what's most important to you. You can make effective decisions for yourself. You've set some goals. As you work toward these goals, you'll have to deal with all sorts of people and situations. Clearly and tactfully communicating to others what you need and expect from them will help you get what you want.

How good are you at communicating your needs? Do you let people know how you're feeling? Or do you expect them to get that information from brain waves, outer space, or your teen-age daughter who's taken to sneaking peeks at your private journal?

Aggressive, Assertive or Passive?

Assertiveness is a method of communication that lets others know your ideas and feelings, while respecting their feelings, as well.

For the purpose of our discussion, behavior can be divided into three types: aggressive, assertive and passive. A person behaving aggressively states her feelings directly, but she violates the rights of others. For example, suppose the chairperson of a committee you are on asks you to design a flyer for the membership mailing within the next two days. You have a husband, two children, and a job outside the home. What you don't have is extra time and a need for additional stress in your life. You say, "Absolutely not. If you can't be organized enough to get things done earlier, you have no business being the chair of this committee." While this may be true, your aggressive response may anger the chairperson. She is not likely to cooperate when you need a favor. An assertive reply would be honest and direct, but not disrespectful. One such response might be, "I'm sorry, but I couldn't possibly fit it into my schedule. If you can give me about two weeks' notice, though, I'd be happy to help out next time." When you respond passively, you avoid immediate conflict, but you may be upset with yourself because you haven't expressed your feelings. A passive response to the situation would be to design the flyers, even though you did not have time, or to decline, by making up some false excuse.

For the following examples, identify each response as:

+ = aggressive
0 = assertive
− = passive

SITUATION 1

Your daughter-in-law asks you to babysit for the third time this week and you don't want to.

Response

_____ If you can't afford a babysitter, you have no business going out.
_____ Yes, I'd love it.
_____ You know I love spending time with the kids, but I've been neglecting my friends and I want to go out with them this evening.

SITUATION 2

Several friends at a party ask you to try drugs, but you don't want to do it.

Response

_____ Well, just this once won't hurt.
_____ You're all crazy. What do you want to do that for?
_____ No thanks, I really don't want to try drugs.

SITUATION 3

A bank teller makes a mistake and gives you too little change.

Response

_____ Do nothing.
_____ What are you trying to do, cheat me?
_____ There seems to be a mistake here. I believe you owe me another $5.00.

SITUATION 4

Even though you've finalized your vacation plans, your mother-in-law insists you change them and come to visit as you do every year.'

Response

_____ This vacation means a great deal to the family. Why don't you plan to come visit us at Christmas instead?
_____ If you cared about us at all, you wouldn't try to make us feel guilty for taking a vacation we could actually enjoy.
_____ You change your plans.

SITUATION 5

Your new supervisor is becoming too familiar and you want to stop his suggestive comments before he goes any further.

Response

_____ I've had it with your continual harrassment. It's men like you who make life miserable for working women.
_____ If you continue this kind of behavior, I'll be forced to bring the matter to your boss's attention.
_____ You grin and bear it.

SITUATION 6

You would like to be nominated for president of a local charitable organization.

Response

_____ I think I am qualified and would like to be nominated for president.
_____ Don't nominate Sarah; she's unqualified.
_____ Think to yourself, "I hope someone nominates me."

SITUATION 7

Your doctor tells you you need a hysterectomy. You are not comfortable with one opinion.

Response

_____ I know you doctors recommend unneeded surgery all the time, just to make more money.
_____ I'll have the surgery.
_____ This is such an important decision, I need to seek a second opinion.

SITUATION 8

You are turned down for a raise you know you deserve.

Response

_____ You feel bad and say nothing.
_____ If you don't give me that raise, I'm going to quit right now.
_____ I feel that I really deserved a raise and would be interested in hearing why you decided not to give it to me.

SITUATION 9

You are talking to a friend and suddenly realize that if you don't leave immediately you'll be late for work. She wants to keep talking.

Response

_____ I really ought to be going.
_____ I'm hanging up right now! You're making me late for work!
_____ I know you want to talk more and we'll get together after work. Bye.

SITUATION 10

Your brother-in-law continues to make sexist remarks.

Response

_____ You chauvinist pig! When will you learn?
_____ I really don't care to hear you make remarks like that, Bill. They are insensitive.
_____ You change the subject and ignore the comments.

Write Your Own Responses

Get the idea? Now try the different roles.

For the following situations, write one aggressive, one assertive and one passive response. An example of each has been done for you.

A salesperson at your door wants you to purchase something you have no use for.

Aggressive: You slam the door.

_____

Assertive: "I'm really not interested, thank you."

_____

Passive: You buy the item.

_____

Your friend asks to borrow your car, and you don't want to lend it.

Aggressive: "No way! Are you kidding?"

_____

Assertive: "I make it a practice not to lend my car to anyone."

_____

Passive: "Drive carefully."

_____

You arrive at a hotel where you have a reservation only to find there is no room available.

Aggressive: _____

_____

Assertive: _____

_____

Passive: _____

_____

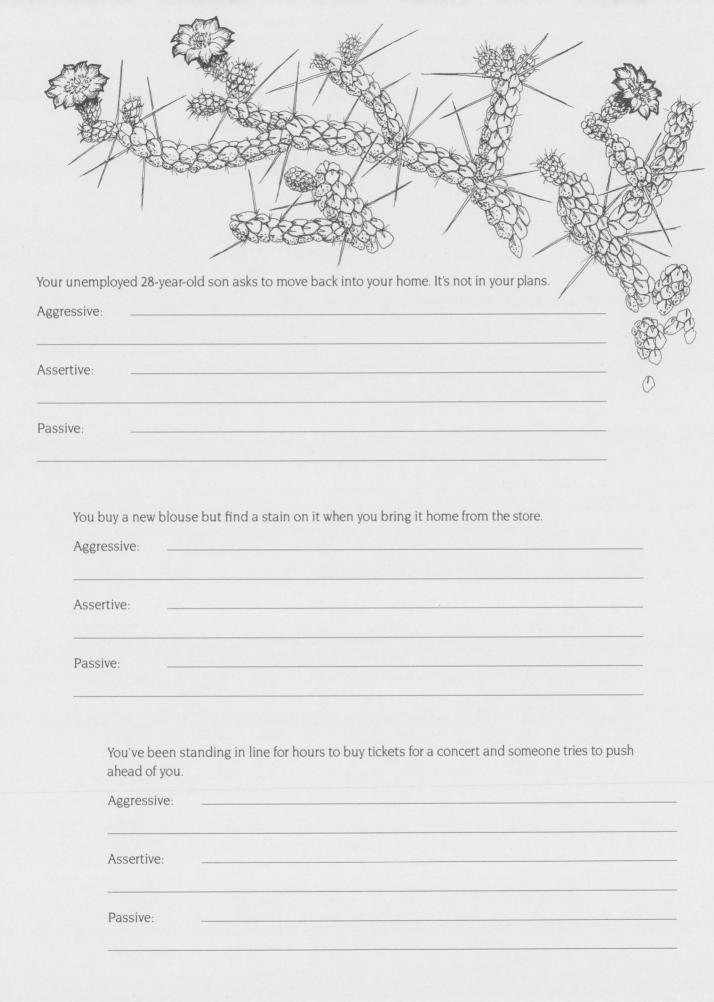

Your unemployed 28-year-old son asks to move back into your home. It's not in your plans.

Aggressive: _____

_____

Assertive: _____

_____

Passive: _____

_____

You buy a new blouse but find a stain on it when you bring it home from the store.

Aggressive: _____

_____

Assertive: _____

_____

Passive: _____

_____

You've been standing in line for hours to buy tickets for a concert and someone tries to push ahead of you.

Aggressive: _____

_____

Assertive: _____

_____

Passive: _____

_____

147

Try to recall situations when you have responded in either an aggressive, assertive, or a passive manner. How did you feel about yourself in each situation?

Aggressive situation: _____
_____
_____

How did you feel? _____
_____
_____

Assertive situation: _____
_____
_____

How did you feel? _____
_____
_____

Passive situation: _____
_____
_____

How did you feel? _____
_____
_____

Truth and Consequences

The way you say things has an effect on those around you. That is why it is not always easy to respond the way you truly want. There are advantages and disadvantages in choosing an assertive, aggressive, or passive response. For example, a person may through passive behavior avoid conflicts, confrontations or risk. Passive behavior, however, may not produce the desired outcome. In the long run, overly passive persons often feel bad about themselves.

Just because you give in to someone else doesn't always mean you've been passive. It could mean you've made a conscious choice in yielding. Or, it could be because you honestly agree with the other person. Being passive refers to consistently doing things you don't really want to do.

Aggressive behavior often produces the desired outcome — at least for the moment. Releasing feelings of anger or frustration can sometimes give a person a sense of control in the situation. If, however, a person continually ignores the feelings of others, she may find herself alone and unliked.

Assertiveness allows individuals to feel good about having expressed their needs, thoughts, or feelings and about making their own choices. Assertive behavior also produces the desired result more frequently than passive behavior. However, self-assertion is not fail-safe. Note the example which follows.

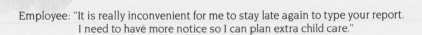

Employee: "It is really inconvenient for me to stay late again to type your report. I need to have more notice so I can plan extra child care."

Response 1: Boss: "You're obviously not on my team. You'll have to find a new job."

Response 2: Boss: "You're right. I will try to plan ahead and give you more notice."

As you can see from the example, assertive responses don't always prevent unpleasant situations. Often you must decide whether or not it is wise to let others know how you feel. In the long run, though, being honest with yourself and others is beneficial to all concerned.

Assertive communication skills take practice, but they can be quite useful. By expressing yourself in ways that don't put down or offend others, you are more likely to make your point. Likewise, making your feelings known, instead of keeping them hidden, lets others know where they stand.

REFLECTIONS

CHAPER SEVEN

So What's New?

Planning for change

Evie had saved for years to start her own business. Now she had enough money, and she was ready to go for it.

After 25 years of marriage, Shirley's husband walked out, and Shirley was left to support herself for the first time in her life.

Lynn had always been a vital, energetic woman. Then she injured her back in an auto accident, and she had to change her entire lifestyle.

Alice had a husband and two grown children she loved, but it wasn't enough, somehow. Sometimes she found herself thinking, "Is this all there is?"

All these woman face change. Sometimes we *choose* to change; other times we have change *forced* upon us. Either way, there is something a little bit frightening about it. We all resist change to some extent.

But change can be exciting, too. Without change, we stop growing. With change, we continue to grow, to dream, and to bring our dreams to fulfillment.

If *you* are currently facing a major change, whether by choice or not, there are things you can do to help make it a positive experience. You will need to evaluate your dreams and your values, as well as the realities of your economic situation. Since it is important to have emotional support for your efforts, you need to identify people or organizations that will be available to you. You need to consider whether or not you have the *energy* to change right now. And you need to plan.

In this chapter, you will identify what it is you need or want to change in your life, and you will develop a plan to accomplish your goal. First, though, it is important to ask yourself how you *feel* about change. The following exercise will help you.

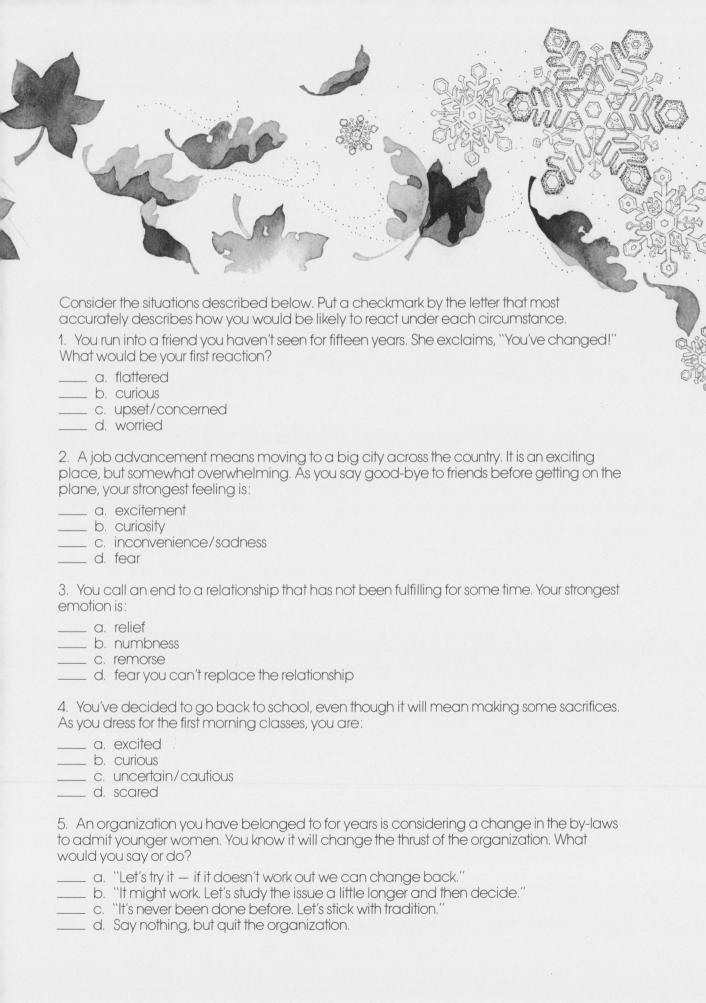

Consider the situations described below. Put a checkmark by the letter that most accurately describes how you would be likely to react under each circumstance.

1. You run into a friend you haven't seen for fifteen years. She exclaims, "You've changed!" What would be your first reaction?

____ a. flattered
____ b. curious
____ c. upset/concerned
____ d. worried

2. A job advancement means moving to a big city across the country. It is an exciting place, but somewhat overwhelming. As you say good-bye to friends before getting on the plane, your strongest feeling is:

____ a. excitement
____ b. curiosity
____ c. inconvenience/sadness
____ d. fear

3. You call an end to a relationship that has not been fulfilling for some time. Your strongest emotion is:

____ a. relief
____ b. numbness
____ c. remorse
____ d. fear you can't replace the relationship

4. You've decided to go back to school, even though it will mean making some sacrifices. As you dress for the first morning classes, you are:

____ a. excited
____ b. curious
____ c. uncertain/cautious
____ d. scared

5. An organization you have belonged to for years is considering a change in the by-laws to admit younger women. You know it will change the thrust of the organization. What would you say or do?

____ a. "Let's try it — if it doesn't work out we can change back."
____ b. "It might work. Let's study the issue a little longer and then decide."
____ c. "It's never been done before. Let's stick with tradition."
____ d. Say nothing, but quit the organization.

Look back at your responses. Which letter did you check most often? Did you check mostly:

a) If most of your responses fell into this category, change is easy for you. You are likely to welcome it. You view life as an adventure, with change as something to be embraced, rather that feared.

b) If you had a majority of responses in this category, you are probably not opposed to change, but you are somewhat more cautious than those who checked mostly "a" responses. You are curious about life, but make changes deliberately. That's fine. You will probably be very comfortable with the planning approach to change described in this chapter.

c) If the majority of your responses fell into this category, you are not really comfortable with change. You would prefer that things remain the way they are. It will be more difficult for you to make changes in your life than it is for some other people, so you will have to make a greater commitment to your goal. Make sure you have an adequate support system to give you encouragement along the way.

d) If most of your responses were in this category, you are likely to find change frightening. That does not mean, however, that you cannot change. In order to become more comfortable with the process, you might start out by making small, short-term changes, or changes that can easily be reversed. Then, when you become more confident or your ability to adjust, you can move on to bigger, more long-term changes. If you have had a major change forced upon you, you may need professional help to guide you through the process.

"How we feel about change, in whatever form, helps to illustrate and define how we see ourselves."
— Sonya Friedman
   Smart Cookies Don't Crumble

"We grow forward when the delights of growth and anxieties of safety are greater than the anxieties of growth and the delights of safety."
— Abraham H. Maslow
   Toward a Psychology of Being

What is it that *you* want to change? There are an endless number of possibilities. Some are easy, others can be overwhelming. Many can be reversed. Almost all can be survived. In order to be successful, however, it is important to define precisely what it is you want to change. Some short- and long-term goals are listed below.

If change is difficult for you, you should probably begin by making some of the easy changes. These can usually be reversed, and the consequences are short-term. Do you think you would like to change your:

Hair style	Bedtime
Car	Route to work
Hobby	Supermarket
Furniture arrangement	Newspaper/magazine
Style of dressing	Perfume
Eating habits	Vacation spot
Waking time	Holiday traditions

Can you think of others? _____

_____

_____

Sooner or later, nearly everyone faces bigger changes, those with long-term consequences. These changes might be brought about by:

Getting married	Retiring
Having children	The death of a loved one
Getting divorced	Financial reverses
Going to work	Financial advances
Going back to school	Changing values
Getting remarried	Changing dreams
Moving to a new city	Parenting your parents
Changing jobs	Grandparenting
Changing careers	Children moving back in
Living with an illness or injury	Getting older

Can you think of others? _____

_____

_____

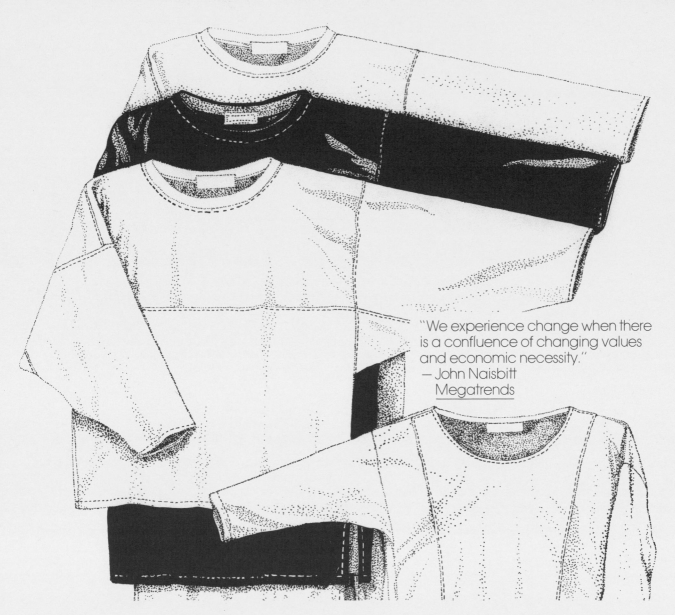

"We experience change when there is a confluence of changing values and economic necessity."
— John Naisbitt
Megatrends

The quote above offers a concise description of the circumstances leading to many changes. Sometimes it involves economic *choice* or *ability* (especially for people who *enjoy* change). But it is usually economic *necessity* that forces change on those who, given the choice, would just as soon have things go on as they are. If you lose your job, or if you suddenly need to support yourself, the choice is removed from you: You *must* change.

Values, too, play an important role in the equation leading to change. You need to be dissatisfied with the way things are, or there is no reason to alter the situation. Sometimes a change in values is obvious: Though you were happy to be a full-time homemaker while your children were young, you now know that what you want is a job outside the home. Or you may not even be aware that your values have changed. You feel dissatisfied with a way of life that once pleased you, but you don't really know why. It is important to rethink your values from time to time, just to make sure you know what they are *now*.

The stories on the following page illustrate the roles economics and values play in the process of change.

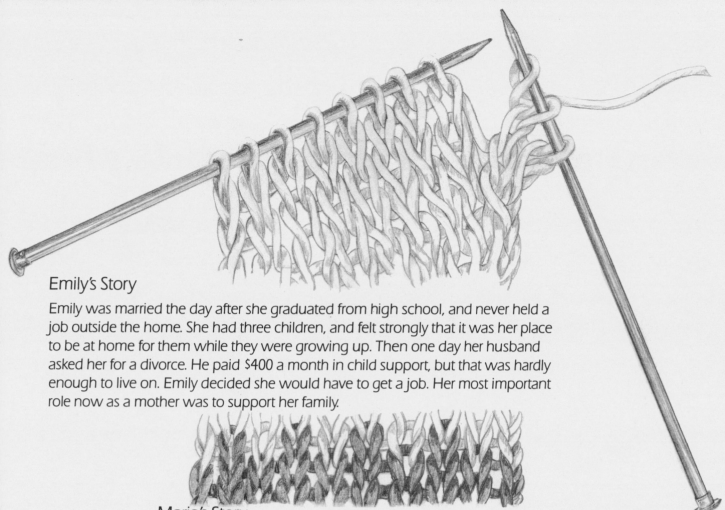

Emily's Story

Emily was married the day after she graduated from high school, and never held a job outside the home. She had three children, and felt strongly that it was her place to be at home for them while they were growing up. Then one day her husband asked her for a divorce. He paid $400 a month in child support, but that was hardly enough to live on. Emily decided she would have to get a job. Her most important role now as a mother was to support her family.

Maria's Story

Maria worked as a real estate agent for twenty years, and was extremely successful at her job. It wasn't as satisfying to her as it had been, however. She wanted to work at something she considered more valuable to society. Maria quit her real estate job and went to work as an advocate for the homeless. The pay was low, but her savings from the real estate job allowed her to make the change to a more satisfying career.

Hortense's Story

Hortense had two grown children, and too much time on her hands. She wanted to do something more with her life, and was also concerned about financial security for her retirement years. Hortense had worked as a volunteer in a number of non-profit organizations, and liked the idea of having a paid position in one of them. She began working toward a degree in business management which, combined with her experience, would make her qualified to direct an agency.

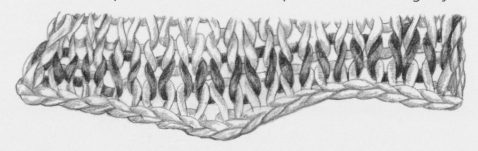

What is it that you are thinking about changing? Describe the situation as it exists today.

_____

_____

_____

What were your values when you entered the situation you now want to change? (See pages 88 to 105 to review values clarification.)

_____

_____

_____

What are your values today? How have they changed?

_____

_____

_____

What was your economic situation then?

_____

_____

_____

What is your economic situation today? How has it changed?

_____

_____

_____

Have your values changed?   Yes   No
Has your economic situation changed?   Yes   No

Consider your responses, then read the following statements. Choose the statement that best describes your situation. If none apply, write your own.

"Because my values and economic situation have changed, I **must** change."

"Because my values and economic situation have changed, I **can** change."

"My values have changed but my economic status will not allow my desired change at this time."

"My values have not changed but my economic situation has. I need to

_____ "

Other: _____

The last statement printed above probably describes the most difficult situation. This is especially true if there has been an economic reversal in your life, one which has been forced upon you. It probably means that you must seek employment. Take some time to reflect on and evaluate your values about work. How realistic are they? You will need to plan carefully to arrange your life so that your financial needs are met and your values are upheld. Or it may mean conscientiously reframing your values as Emily did.

Emily's goal - **To be a good mother**
Value changed from: **A mother's place is to be at home available for her children**
to
A mother's place is to be able to support her children.

159

Getting Support for Change

Making a major life change is a difficult process, but one that can be greatly eased with the proper support. The most essential form of support comes from yourself. You need enough self-esteem so that you believe you *deserve* to have a satisfying life, along with confidence in your ability to change.

It is also helpful if the people you care about — your family and close friends — support your effort to change. Unfortunately, this is often not the case. Sometimes it suits other people's purposes to have you remain the same: A husband who is used to having dinner on the table when he gets home from work may not be happy about your desire to get an outside job that would force him to fend for himself occasionally. Sometimes others are threatened by your change: It might make an overweight friend face her own situation if you are successful in losing weight.

Before you go to them for support, evaluate the situation carefully. What are their expectations of you? If you change, what will happen to their expectations? Can you be reasonably sure that they will be supportive? If not, it might be better to look elsewhere for reinforcement of your decision.

You might find the support you need from peers or colleagues who have faced similar changes: A divorced woman may be more helpful in seeing you through your marriage dissolution than a close friend who thinks any marriage is better than no marriage at all. Or you might want to join a support group. Alcoholics Anonymous was probably the first group to organize around the principle that people with the same kind of problem can be helpful to each other, but these groups are now available for people going through most kinds of changes.

Perhaps you need or would prefer to have a professional counselor or therapist. These people offer private, concentrated attention on you and your situation. Their experience and training can make them extremely helpful. They can refer you to other professionals or agencies, help you assess your skills and interests, give you information on going back to school or applying for jobs, or offer alternative solutions you may not have thought of. They will listen to you without making judgments, yet they don't let you get sidetracked— they keep you moving toward your goal.

You might also find spiritual support in your religion, or in your own mind and conscience. Feeling at peace with your decision can be a powerful source of courage and determination.

Above all, believe in yourself. No one knows better who you are or what you need.

Use the chart below to evaluate the support you have or need to make your change.

	Your expectations	Their expectations
Family	_____	_____
Friends	_____	_____
Peers/colleagues	_____	_____
Support groups	_____	_____
Therapists	_____	_____
Spiritual/Inner voice	_____	_____

Physical and Emotional Energy for Change

Change takes a great deal of energy, both physical and emotional. As psychologist Clare Graves put it, "Few things are harder to break than old bonds, old views, old prejudices, old convictions, old loves." Do you have the necessary reserves to follow through on your desired change at this time? Use the following quiz to evaluate yourself. CAUTION: It is imperative that you be totally honest as you answer these questions. Overestimating your physical and emotional stamina is dangerous to your health. And *underestimating* may be an avoidance tactic, a way of delaying a change that can make a positive difference in your life.

1. The change I am considering is
    a. my choice. It is a dream of mine.
    b. something I feel I should do. It will improve my sense of well-being.
    c. something that has been forced upon me. Circumstances dictate that I make this change.

2. Which of the following most accurately describes your current health?
    a. I am in excellent physical shape.
    b. I am sick occasionally, but it doesn't get in my way.
    c. My health is a constant complaint.

3. At this time my physical energy level could best be described as:
    a. high. I feel I have the energy I need to make my change..
    b. medium. I run out of energy from time to time, but I can usually muster what I need.
    c. low. I barely make it through the day.

4. At this time my emotional stability could best be described as:
    a. hardy. I can handle detours, criticism and failure all in stride, as part of the process of change.
    b. average. Detours, criticism and failure may slow me down, but I'll probably bounce back.
    c. fragile. If crossed, I'll either blow up, cry or hide.

5. Right now I feel:
    a. very confident. I can handle most situations.
    b. confident most of the time, especially when I know what's expected of me.
    c. not in control of my own destiny. Other people and situations are dictating my future.

Evaluate yourself. Did you identify with more a, b or c answers? Read on for explanations of each category. If you chose the "a" response for most questions, go for it! You're ready to make your action plan for change (see pages 162 to 165). If most of your responses were marked "b," you should be able to proceed with your plan, but be sure to get the support you need, and to plan carefully. If you chose the "c" response for most questions, stop and reassess your plan. Your first goal should be to recover your confidence, health and energy. In the next exercise, make your action plan around this initial phase of the change process. Keep in mind that you may need professional help in order to accomplish the *essential* goal. If change has been forced upon you, you may be suffering from a clinical depression or burn out, conditions that can be treated.

Action Plan for Change

Now that you have carefully examined your situation, it's time to start planning for action. In this exercise, you will use the skills you've learned throughout the book to set up a plan that will help you make your change successfully. Then it will be up to you to put your plan to work.

First turn back to page 153 to review your feelings about change. Write a statement about your feelings below.

_____

_____

_____

What is it you want to or need to change?

_____

_____

_____

What were your values when you made the choice that led to your present situation? (See page 97 to review.)

_____

_____

_____

What are your values now?

_____

_____

_____

Have your values changed?

_____

_____

_____

What was your economic situation when you made the choice that led to your present situation?

_____

_____

_____

What is your economic situation today?

_____

_____

_____

Turn back to page 159 and review the statement you chose concerning your values and finances. Copy that statement below.

_____

_____

_____

Chances are, you have a number of possible ways to accomplish your change. In order to make the best decision for you, complete the chart below. If you need to review how it's done, turn back to pages 120 to 123.

Alternatives	Advantages	Disadvantages

Considering the advantages and disadvantages for each of your alternatives, what is the best choice for you now? Write it below.

_____

_____

_____

Now that you've made your choice, you can set an attainable goal. Turn back to pages 106 to 109 if you need help writing goals; then write yours below.

_____

_____

_____

Can you think of problems, detours or pitfalls that might stand in your way (family or friends who don't want you to change, for example, or a momentary lapse of courage on your part)? How will you assert your right to have the kind of life you will find most satisfying? Write some assertive statements you could use to convince yourself and others that you will not be detoured. Review pages 143 to 149 if you need to.

_____

_____

_____

What skills will you need to make your change successfully? Enter them here.

_____

_____

_____

Which of those skills do you already possess? (See chapter 8 for more on skills identification.)

_____

_____

_____

Which skills do you need to obtain? Remember to include learning these skills in your action plan.

_____

_____

_____

Where will you get the support you need to accomplish your change? Write the names of people or organizations you think would be helpful for you.

Family _____

Friends _____

Peers/Colleagues _____

Support groups _____

Professionals _____

Religious or spiritual organizations _____

Look back to page 160 to see how you evaluated your health and energy level. What did you say?

_____

_____

_____

How, specifically, are you going to accomplish your change? This is your action plan. As you write your objectives, it may be helpful to diagram them. See page 110 for review.

In order to accomplish your goal, what do you need to do immediately?

_____

_____

_____

What do you need to do in the next week?

_____

_____

_____

What do you need to do in the next month?

_____

_____

_____

What are your long-term (one month to three years) objectives?

_____

_____

_____

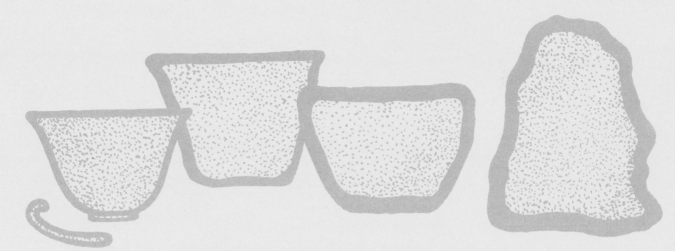

Belinda's Dilemma

Like most women of her generation, Belinda grew up planning to be a full-time homemaker. After college she married Eric, and the young couple bought a home in the suburbs, a station wagon and a dog. They began their family immediately, and by the time Belinda was thirty years old, she was the mother of three. Eric commuted each day to his job in the city, and Belinda spent her day caring for the house and the children, driving the kids from one activity to another, and doing some volunteer work for the local hospital.

Then things began to change. Inflation drove the cost of living way up, and the family had a hard time making ends meet on Eric's income alone. It was time to start saving for the children's college education, too, but that seemed out of the question. Belinda was also beginning to feel cut off from the world—the kids didn't seem to need her as much as they had in the past, and Eric spent a lot of time at the office. She thought about getting a job, talked it over with the family, and went out to see what she could do.

With her college degree and volunteer experience at the hospital, she was able to get a job in the hospital administrator's office. Belinda was elated with her new responsibilities, and took them all very seriously, often working more than the required eight hours a day. She didn't want to be unfair to her family either, of course, so she would rush home to make a big dinner, spend her evenings frantically cleaning and doing laundry, and then collapse into bed.

She knew that something had to change, but she wasn't sure what.

A Changing Society

Like Belinda, millions of women are currently trying to balance their careers and their family life. In fact, the wholesale entrance of American women into the workforce has been hailed as a *revolution* in the way we live.

Women work for many reasons. Inflation and rising prices often make it necessary for a family to have two incomes in order to buy a home, or just to live comfortably. There are also more unmarried women and single parents needing to support themselves than ever before. Other women work simply because they enjoy it, they have a contribution to make to the world, and they find work a satisfying way to accomplish their goals.

While many changes have been made for women in the workforce, things at home have remained substantially the same: The woman does the majority of housework and child care in most families. As a result many women now find themselves with *two* jobs— one outside and one inside the home.

This is not fair, and it is not healthy. Like other people, women need time to eat, sleep and exercise and time to themselves, as well. If you are caught in this bind of having too much to do and not enough time, there are changes you can— you *must*— make. Consider some of the following:

Lower your housekeeping standards. The world will not come crashing down if the beds aren't made every day.

Get help from other family members. They can probably do more than you think they can.

If you can afford it, hire outside help to do tasks you don't have time for.

If you can afford it, cut back your hours on the job.

Find a job with flexible hours, or one you can do at home.

Find a job that pays more so you don't have to work as many hours.

Analyze your own situation. Can you think of other ways it might be changed?

_____

_____

_____

_____

_____

For more ideas see *More Choices: A Strategic Planning Guide for Mixing Career and Family* by Mindy Bingham and Sandy Stryker, page 240.

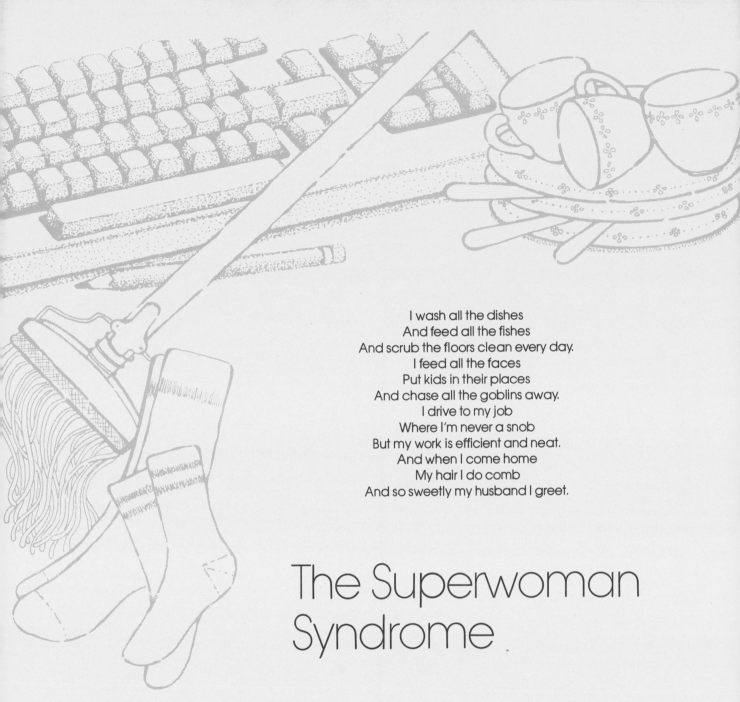

I wash all the dishes
And feed all the fishes
And scrub the floors clean every day.
I feed all the faces
Put kids in their places
And chase all the goblins away.
I drive to my job
Where I'm never a snob
But my work is efficient and neat.
And when I come home
My hair I do comb
And so sweetly my husband I greet.

The Superwoman Syndrome

How realistic is that picture? Can you really "have it all now"? Judging from TV and the movies, "Superwoman" is alive and well. You know the one, the fashionably dressed, perfectly made-up mother of four who runs a million-dollar business in her spare time. That is, when she's not lecturing at Harvard, advising Congress on how to avert national disaster or appearing on a TV talk show to tell us all how to use our food processors during natural childbirth. Of course, she wouldn't *think* of letting her husband help with the housework.

Well, there is no such woman. Thank goodness! You cannot have everything, do everything, and be everything, all at the same time. Priorities have to be set. Working mothers need help from their families. They may have to accept the fact that their homes will not always pass the "white glove test." Maintaining a strong marriage, happy and healthy kids, and a career you enjoy are realistic goals as long as you keep in mind that things will never be perfect.

Even if your children are grown, it is important to set priorities. If you don't, it's easy to get sidetracked. You may find yourself spending your time at things you don't really care about, while your real priorities are given short shrift.

Setting Priorities and Making Time

If you can't have *everything*, what can you have? Well, what do you want? What do you want *most*? It might be painful to find that "you're only human," but at least you have the power to decide which things are most important to you. Then you can make those goals your top priorities — the things you'll try hardest for, put ahead of other interests, spend the most time on. It's possible to have hundreds of accomplishments and still find yourself unsatisfied, simply because you never made time to do the one thing you most wanted. The next exercise will help you decide what your priorities are and where your time can best be spent.

"Superwoman's" list of activities has already been completed. After reading it, use the spaces provided to make a list of all the things you have to do or would like to do in the following week. Include housework, outside jobs, relationships, activities with friends, whatever you usually do. Then, beside each entry, indicate its importance to you. Many factors contribute to how "important" each task is. For example, attending a meeting may not be *personally* important to you, but cooperating with your employer's requests may be.

For each task or activity, indicate its importance by writing an "A", "B", or "C". Place an "A" by activities that *have* to get done in the next week or are of most importance for you personally. You will sacrifice some things for these. They are your top priorities. Then write a "B" by activities that are important, but not crucial. Write a "C" by items that would be nice to get done if you have time, but won't cause problems if they are left undone.

After you have listed your "A", "B", and "C" priorities, try to work on your "A's" first and complete them before going on to the "B's". Then finally, if you have the time, do your "C" tasks.

Our fictitious (and over-extended) "Superwoman's" list might look something like this:

Return proofs of new book to publisher	— A	Take flying lesson	— B
Interview with Barbara Walters	— A	Cammie's Little League game	— A
Change oil on Mercedes	— C	Run in Boston Marathon	— A
Conference with kids' teachers	— A	Weed vegetable garden	— B
Dinner with John Travolta	— B	Repair home computer	— B
Clean toilets	— C	Paint mural on front hall wall	— C
Read newspaper	— C	Iron sheets	— C
Testify before Senate committee	— A	Wax no-wax floor	— C
Bake brownies	— C	Start research for new book	— B
Sew costume for Muffy	— A	Romantic evening with Tom	— A
Attend exercise class	— C	Sleep	— C

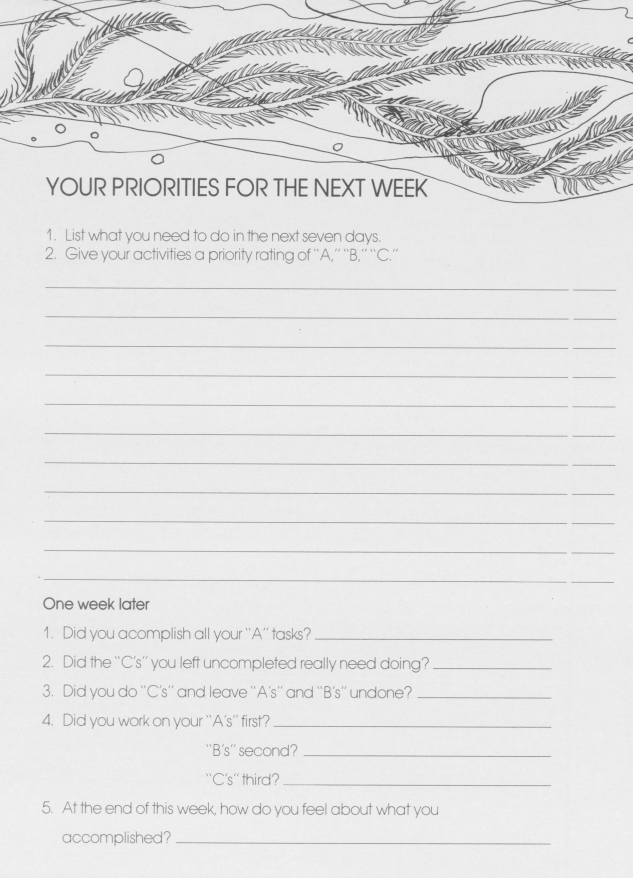

YOUR PRIORITIES FOR THE NEXT WEEK

1. List what you need to do in the next seven days.
2. Give your activities a priority rating of "A," "B," "C."

_____ _____

_____ _____

_____ _____

_____ _____

_____ _____

_____ _____

_____ _____

_____ _____

_____ _____

_____ _____

One week later

1. Did you acomplish all your "A" tasks? _____

2. Did the "C's" you left uncompleted really need doing? _____

3. Did you do "C's" and leave "A's" and "B's" undone? _____

4. Did you work on your "A's" first? _____

    "B's" second? _____

    "C's" third? _____

5. At the end of this week, how do you feel about what you

   accomplished? _____

A list like this allows you to plan your time more effectively, achieve the things that are most important to achieve at the time, and helps you avoid procrastination of an important, but maybe unpleasurable activity.

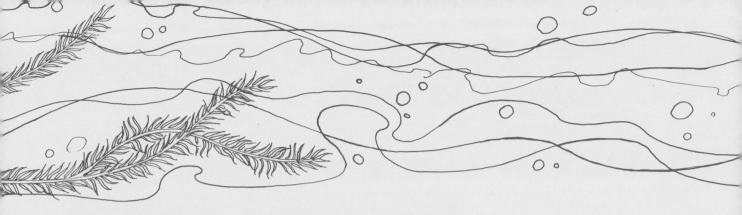

YOUR PRIORITIES FOR THE NEXT MONTH

1. List what you need to do during the next month.
2. Give your activities a priority rating of "A," "B," "C."

_____

_____

_____

_____

_____

_____

_____

_____

_____

_____

_____

_____

_____

_____

_____

_____

_____

_____

_____

_____

_____

_____

_____

_____

REFLECTIONS

CHAPTER EIGHT

What Can You Do?

Skills identification

If you don't know where you're
going . . . you're there.

Sarah Crocker's Story

"I don't know what to do," said Sarah Crocker to her friend Louise. "I'm supposed to identify all my skills for my career planning course, and it makes me feel like such a loser! I mean, I can't do anything! Want another piece of cheesecake?"

"Sure," said Louise. "This is great stuff!"

"Thanks. I've got about a zillion of them here. My club is having its annual bazaar tomorrow, and people have been calling all week to reserve them. I made a bunch last year, and they were sold out in about five minutes. So I've been making cheesecake for days, and I haven't even had time to think about my skills. My list is due Monday. Mrs. Johnson is going to kill me!"

Sometimes it's hard to see the obvious. Fortunately for Sarah Crocker, her career counselor, Mrs. Johnson, arrived at the bazaar early enough to buy one of Sarah's cheesecakes, and launched her on a very successful career. Sarah Crocker Frozen Cheesecakes are now available in all fifty states and twenty countries. Sarah is currently negotiating a contract to distribute them in China.

What about you and your skills? If you've thought about them at all, you've probably underestimated yourself. Whether you're making a cheesecake or solving a math problem, everything you do involves a skill. And, for most people, what you do with your life depends on what you do well.

It's time to start looking at yourself in terms of what you like to do and what you are able to do. A word of caution here, before you start. This won't work unless you're realistic. *No one person is good at everything, nor is there any person devoid of all skills.* Strengths and weaknesses vary from person to person. There are over 20,000 different jobs. Some of them are right for you.

If you aren't successful at making things, if solving math problems is frustrating and takes you a long time, if you can't run fast, whatever your weaknesses are, take a minute to ask yourself why you have difficulty with some tasks. Is a lack of experience or ignorance the problem? Or is this simply not one of your strengths?

If you honestly feel you don't have the aptitude to be really good at something, don't feel that you should give it up entirely. If it's something you enjoy, that's great. Keep it up. It's smart to avoid trying to make a living at a job that requires a skill you simply don't have. With that caution, it's time to look at what you can do.

What Are Your Skills?

Like many people, when Miranda thought about skills, she thought of things like designing computers or playing tennis with both legs tied together, using a shovel instead of a racquet, as she had seen on TV. (Now there's a skill!) She never considered the things she did every day as skills. But in a typical day she might make a Halloween costume for her three-year-old, fix a toaster, write a report at work, balance her checkbook, ask for a raise in a forceful and diplomatic way, prepare a new recipe for dinner, and convince five other women to make cookies for the holiday bazaar. All of Miranda's activities involve skills. And so do *your* activities. Not only do you already know how to do hundreds of things, but you have the potential to learn many more.

As you go through your day, jot down the things that you do and the skills that they involve. You may be surprised at the variety of your talents. Use the following exercise to help identify them.

List as many of your activities as you can think of (cooking, fixing a flat tire, decorating a home, balancing a budget, gardening, playing golf, etc.) on the chart which follows.

What kinds of skills are involved in each activity? Record them in the "Skills" column on the chart.

Next, think about what it is that you *like* about each of the activities. Do you enjoy playing golf because you're good at it? Because you like being outdoors in a pleasant setting? Some other reasons? List your likes in the "What Do You Like About This Activity?" column on the chart.

In what *environment* are the activities conducted? Indoors? With people? Alone? List the environments in the "Environment" column on the chart.

Activities	Skills	What Do You Like About This Activity?	Environment

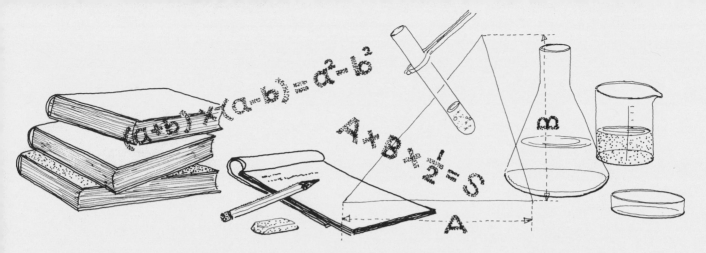

What about school? What were your best subjects? Your worst? What was your favorite? Why? Make sure your reactions are to the *subject*, not just to a teacher you particularly liked or disliked. If you're not really sure what you like, you might want to take an interest inventory test. A career counselor at your community college should be able to help you with this. An interest inventory is a quick-answer test that, when evaluated, helps give insight into where your interests lie. You may discover some interests you haven't considered at all.

Best subjects: _____

_____

_____

Why?: _____

_____

_____

_____

Worst subjects: _____

_____

_____

Why?: _____

_____

_____

_____

Favorite subjects: _____

_____

_____

Why?: _____

_____

_____

_____

Job Skills

All jobs require some skills. The ability to work quickly with numbers or information is required by many jobs. Being able to talk to people, to influence them or supervise them is an important skill in many occupations. The ability to maneuver an earth-mover or operate a complicated machine is still another skill area required by many jobs. One could say that some jobs require "people skills," others rely more on manual dexterity and working with things, and still others require manipulating numbers, data or ideas. Miranda's convincing the other women to bake cookies is a "people skill" as is asking for a raise. Fixing the toaster, making dinner, and sewing the costume are skills that deal with things. Writing the report and balancing the checkbook show that Miranda can manipulate data, ideas, and numbers, as well.

Look back at your own list of skills. Do they seem to be more prevalent in one or two areas? Do you have a preference for dealing with people? Information? Things? When you learn something new, ask yourself how it relates to a skill. If you seem to come up with a number of skills that involve talking with people, and if you enjoy it, that can be a valuable clue as to what your career might be. What kinds of jobs involve talking with people? A marriage counselor, a psychologist, or a principal are a few possible choices. Use the types of skills that stand out on your own list and think of as many jobs as you can that might relate to each. For example, Miranda's persuasive abilities could indicate that she'd be good at selling real estate, as well. Or her diplomacy could be developed into a job with the foreign service. What about your skills?

_____

_____

_____

_____

_____

_____

_____

_____

_____

_____

Experience What You Can

If you still think your list of skills looks a little sparse, don't worry. There are thousands of things you haven't had a chance to experience yet. It's not too soon to start. The more experiences you have, the better able you'll be to make career decisions. The opportunities are there. There are sports to be played, organizations to be joined, and unusual classes to be taken. If you live in a city, visit its museums and theatres. Volunteer jobs can provide a wide variety of experiences. Work on a political campaign. Get to know people of different ages and cultural backgrounds, and learn from them. Even if you tend to be shy, joining a club or taking part in activities will put you in contact with other people who have similar interests. You'll find that the more things you try, the bolder you will become. The whole world will open up to you!

If you're particularly attracted to a certain environment (the beach, a hospital), spend time there. Look around. What are people doing on the job? Do any of the jobs appeal to you? Be bold! Ask questions! Your future and security could depend on it!

REFLECTIONS

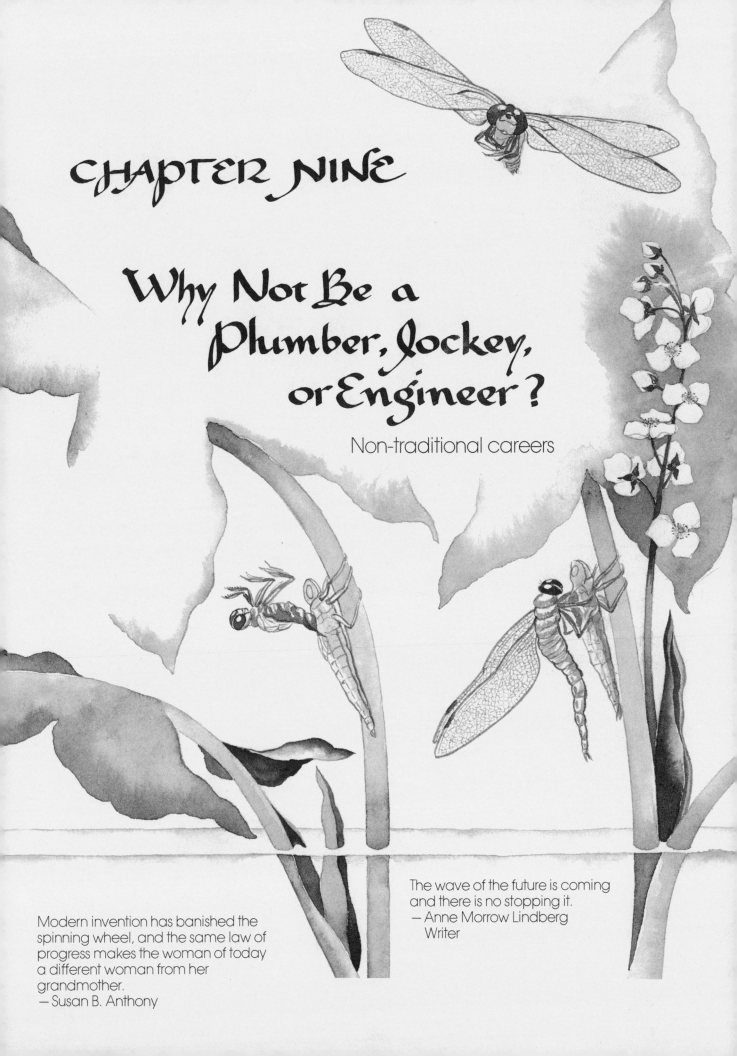

CHAPTER NINE

Why Not Be a Plumber, Jockey, or Engineer?

Non-traditional careers

Modern invention has banished the spinning wheel, and the same law of progress makes the woman of today a different woman from her grandmother.
— Susan B. Anthony

The wave of the future is coming and there is no stopping it.
— Anne Morrow Lindberg
   Writer

Rose's Story

Once upon a time, before there were microwave ovens or acrylic fingernails, there lived a girl named Rose. One day, she bravely announced to all her friends who were planning to be secretaries, "I want to be a plumber."

"A plumber!" exclaimed her father. "What kind of job is that for a girl? You'll get dirty! You'll hurt yourself!"

"It can't be any nastier than changing diapers," said Rose, who had been babysitting for years. "I have the ability. I want to do it." She raised her voice for emphasis, and would not change her mind, even when her father offered bribes of cashmere sweaters and a trip to Hawaii.

"A plumber!" cried her mother. "What will people say? Why can't you be nice like your cousin Ruth who's doing so well as a typist, and gets to wear high heels and earrings and to make coffee for all those important men at the bank?"

"I'd rather make money than coffee," insisted Rose, as she refused to change her mind and handed her mother a handkerchief for her tears. "It'll be all right, Mom. Someday you'll be proud of me."

And Rose was right. After starting work as a plumber, she not only felt she was doing what she wanted, but soon she was making over $13 an hour. Later, she started her own business, and before long, had several franchises. Pink "Plumbing by Rose" vans could be seen making house calls in towns throughout her part of the country. Soon after, Rose bought herself a sports car and sent her parents on a trip to Hawaii.

Cousin Ruth, in the meantime, was still wearing high heels and earrings to her job at the bank, where she was still making the coffee—and still making less than a quarter of what Rose made when she started.

Thanks to Rose and lots of other brave women, it is easier for you to work as a plumber, lawyer, pilot, or anything else that not so long ago you had to be a man to be. It still may not be *easy* to pursue such careers, but the ice has been broken in most fields. You will probably never have to be "The First Woman" anything. (If your heart is set on being the first woman in some particular occupation, however, there are still a few career choices remaining. President of the United States is one you may want to tackle.)

Why should you consider careers that have been traditionally held by men? There are a couple of good reasons. The first is that in general, you will be able to make more money at them. Look back at your budget. It costs a lot to support yourself today. Many of the so-called "women's jobs" just do not pay enough for a person to live on.

And secondly, you may find "male" jobs as interesting and fulfilling as many of the men who hold them do. Just like men, you have talents and abilities of different kinds. Why shouldn't you be able to put them to use in the way that will make you happiest? You owe it to yourself to consider *all* possibilities before you make your career choices.

Ask a Career Woman

If you are considering entering or re-entering the work force or making a career change, one of the best ways to gather information is the interview technique. What do the working women you know think about career choices? Interview two who are close to you, using these questions as a guide.

First Interview

Person interviewed _____

Job Title _____ Date _____

Why did you choose the career you did?

_____

_____

_____

What has been the most satisfying part of your job?

_____

_____

_____

What has been the least satisfying, or the most frustrating part of your job?

_____

_____

_____

If you had to do it over, would you choose the same job?

_____

If not, what other choice would you make?

_____

As I start preparing myself for a career or a career change, what advice would you give me?

_____

_____

_____

Second Interview

Person interviewed _____

Job Title _____ Date _____

Why did you choose the career you did?

_____

_____

_____

What has been the most satisfying part of your job?

_____

_____

_____

What has been the least satisfying, or the most frustrating, part of your job?

_____

_____

_____

If you had to do it over, would you choose the same job?

_____

If not, what other choice would you make?

_____

As I start preparing myself for a career or a career change, what advice would you give me?

_____

_____

_____

IMPORTANT FIRSTS

Women have made many advances in recent years. The following table lists just a few of their "firsts." New "firsts" are now less common, because so many women have entered careers that were formerly thought to be "for men only."

SOME FEMALE FIRSTS

First woman to pilot a jet plane	Ann Baumgartner 1947
First woman U.S. Supreme Court Justice	Sandra O'Connor 1981
First woman vice-presidential candidate	Geraldine Ferraro 1984
First American woman astronaut	Sally Ride 1983
First woman Formula 1 race driver	Lella Lombardi 1974
First widely syndicated cartoon-strip by a woman artist ("Brenda Starr")	Dale Messik 1940
First Olympic athlete to score a perfect 10.00 in any event	Nadia Comaneci 1976
First person to receive seven perfect scores as a gymnast	Nadia Comaneci 1976
First woman to receive the Nobel Prize for physics	Marie Curie 1903
First person to win two Nobel Prizes with the Nobel Prize for chemistry	Marie Curie 1911
First woman to climb Mt. Everest	Junko Tabei 1975
First woman to sail solo around the world	Naomi James 1978
First woman to conduct the Metropolitan Opera	Sarah Caldwell 1976
First woman state governor	Nellie Tayloe Ross 1924
First woman airplane designer	Lillian Todd 1906
First woman dentist (officially earned degree)	Lucy B. Hobbs 1866
First woman foreign correspondent (Chicago Daily News)	Helen Kirkpatrick 1939
First woman president of the United Nations General Assembly	Vijayalakshmi Pandid 1953
First woman to receive the Nobel Prize for Literature	Selma Lagerlof 1909
First woman pilot to fly solo across the Atlantic	Amelia Earhart 1928
First American woman to win three gold medals at the Olympics in track and field	Wilma Rudolph 1960
First computer programmer	Ada Augusta Lovelace 1915
First woman to orbit the earth	Valentina Tereshkova-Nikolayeva 1963
First woman to own a baseball team (New York Mets)	Joan Whitney Payson 1962
First woman to win major Pulitzer Prize in Journalism	Anne O'Hare McCormick 1937
First woman boxing referee	Carol Polis 1973

Stereotypes Persist

One of the most amazing things about women who first moved into non-traditional careers is that they did so without female role models, and in the face of widespread social disapproval. You are fortunate to have women as role models now, but the old stereotypes have not disappeared.

Trudy's Story

Trudy discovered this when she decided to be an engineer. It was more difficult to be accepted into a college program than she thought it should have been, considering her excellent grades. When classes began, she found she was the only woman in some of her classes. All of her instructors were men. During lab, it seemed as if everyone was watching her, waiting for her to make a mistake. There didn't seem to be any women engineers on TV or in the movies. There certainly weren't any in the fashion magazines she read for relaxation.

Trudy began to feel like some kind of freak, and wondered if she wouldn't be better off as a teacher. But when she re-examined her values and personal goals, she realized that engineering held more rewards for her. She decided to stick with engineering, and is now glad she did. She feels it was unfair that she had to prove herself to her co-workers, simply because she was a woman; since she's shown them that she can work just as hard and just as well as they can, she's earned their respect. She loves her job and the financial security it provides.

Money Counts

Louise's Story

Louise enjoyed working with numbers, and knew she wanted that to be part of her job. But she wasn't sure if she should take a two-year vocational course to become a bookkeeper, or a college program, which would allow her to become an accountant. Louise looked up both jobs in the Occupational Outlook Handbook at the library. She was surprised to learn that, as a bookkeeper, she could expect to start at less than $12,000 a year. As an accountant, she could start at about $19,000. If she went on to obtain certification as a public accountant, her earnings would be even greater. Louise decided accounting was the field for her.

Often, women think about a skill they have or the amount of training they want or can afford, and then automatically choose a traditional "woman's job." It's considered "safer" to take a traditional job, but taking a small risk can increase earning power greatly. By thinking just a bit more, women might see that there are other jobs in the same field that require no more training — and that pay *much more*.

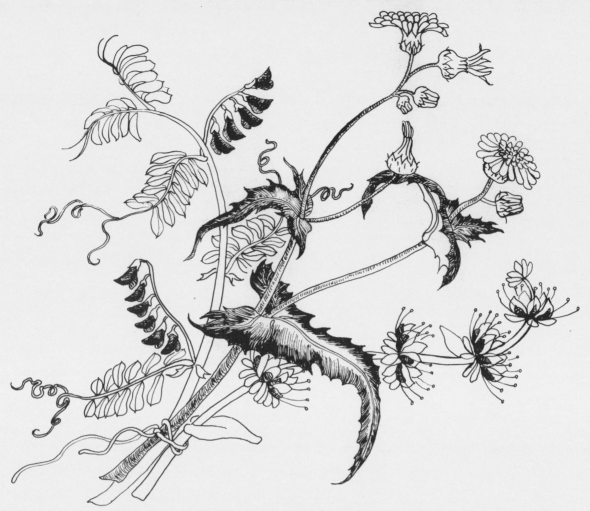

It has only recently been acknowledged that many women work because they need money. In the past many people thought that women should only work until they married. If they worked after marriage, it was assumed that their salaries went only for "extras" or "luxuries." By pretending that women didn't have to support themselves or their families, employers could justify paying them less than men. Although we now know that women work for the same reasons that men do, the pattern remains: Jobs which have traditionally been held by women continue to pay less than comparable jobs which are usually held by men. That's one reason why you should consider a "man's job": You are quite likely to earn more money in a non-traditional career. If you love to travel or fly, for example, you have probably considered becoming a flight attendant. In that job, you could expect to start at a salary of $13,000 a year, working up to an average of $23,000 a year. But have you thought of becoming a pilot? Commercial airline pilots make up to $80,000 a year by age 50. Of course, it takes more training, more commitment, greater risk and different skills to become a pilot, but how do you know you couldn't do it?

Let's consider a few more examples. A cosmetologist makes on the average about $250-$400 a week, while a plumber can earn up to $585 a week. A person working as a bank teller earns $11,000 a year; a mail carrier can expect to earn $25,000 a year. A typist averages $15,000, while a tool and die maker can make $23,000. A sales clerk will probably start at $3.35 an hour working up to an average of $288 per week. Wholesale trade salesworkers can earn $450 per week.

Beginning to see the pattern? Figures on these and thousands of other occupations are available from the *Occupational Outlook Handbook,* a volume published by the U.S. Department of Labor, and available at your local library. It will tell you not only how much you can expect to be paid for various jobs, but what kind of training is required, and whether or not there is a demand for people in that field. Next time you're at the library, ask to see it. It can be extremely helpful in making career decisions.

Where the Women are, the Money Isn't

Like it or not (and who could like it?), there is a connection between the number of women in various professional careers, and the salaries for those careers. Although plain old sex discrimination plays a part in the difference between what men and women earn, so does the type of career most women *choose*. The following table shows the percentage of women in different fields.[10]

Careers	Percentage of Women
Secretary	99.1
Nurse	94.4
Bank teller	92.9
Cosmetologist	83.3
Librarian	84.6
Elementary teacher	82.4
Doctor	22.8
Lawyer	20.2
Architect	13.3
Engineer	5.9
Truck driver	1.5
Electrician	1.7

Now let's see what the average salary is for each career.

Careers	Salaries
Secretary	$17,000
Nurse (RN)	$21,000
Bank teller	$11,000
Cosmetologist	$17,000
College librarian (with Master's Degree)	$26,000
Elementary teacher	$23,000
Physician	$108,500
Lawyer (private practice with experience)	$88,000
Architect	$29,000
Engineer	$41,000
Truck driver	$25,000
Electrician	$23,000

The Importance of Math

Hilary's Story

In grade school, Hilary was a whiz at math. So were many of the other girls. At times when many of the boys were squirming at their desks, wrinkling their foreheads, and trying to count on their toes, Hilary and the girls had already finished the assignment and had moved on to the extra credit questions and puzzles. Her parents hardly noticed when she brought home A's in math. It happened so often that they just took it for granted.

Then, sometime in junior high school, all that changed. Like her friends, Hilary seemed to lose interest in math. Her grades dropped, but she didn't really care. The boys, on the other hand, seemed to have finally caught on. They were taking all the math offered and doing well in it now. Hilary, on the other hand, stopped taking math classes as soon as she could.

When she entered college, she thought about majoring in business. Then she found she didn't have enough high school math credits. She could have made them up, but somehow the thought of going back to math made her uneasy. She decided to major in literature instead. She wouldn't need math for that.

What happened to Hilary has happened to millions of women. It is called "math anxiety," and it is keeping many women out of higher-paying careers. No one knows exactly why it occurs. One likely theory holds that young women don't feel it is socially acceptable for them to do well in math, or to be interested in the subject, and so they lose interest and eventually drop out. The little girl who loved reciting her multiplication tables can easily become the woman who can't balance her checkbook.

The fact is, you need a math background for many desirable careers. Three years of high school math will give you more career options than almost any other subject. A great array of clerical jobs in banking, insurance, business, and government needs workers with math skills.

If you do not have that math background, it's not too late to get it. There are adult education classes and remedial classes at many community and four-year colleges. You could take a correspondence course, or find a tutor who can give you private lessons.

If you're planning to go to college, a year of algebra and one of geometry are the minimum you'll need. If you have any interest in science or engineering, you ought to take trigonometry and calculus, too. Many colleges will not *admit* you without a solid math background. Whatever your major, one thing is certain. A knowledge of math helps you think analytically, which is an asset in any job.

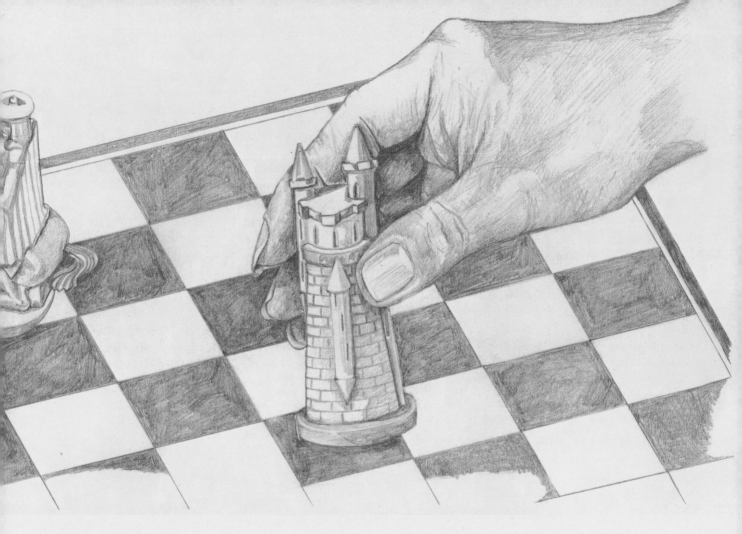

Below is a list of some of the more common college majors. The "yes" or "no" beside each one indicates whether or not some college math is required for a degree in that major.

Major		Major	
Anthropology	— no	Engineering	— yes
Architecture	— yes	English	— no
Art History	— no	French	— no
Astronomy	— yes	History	— no
Biology	— yes	Journalism	— no
Business	— yes	Mathematics	— no
Chemistry	— yes	Music	— no
Classics	— no	Pharmacology	— yes
Computer Science	— yes	Philosophy	— yes
Earth Science	— yes	Physics	— yes
Economics	— yes	Political Science	— no
Environmental Studies	— yes	Psychology	— yes
Education	— no	Sociology	— no

Looking back at the list, you'll see that most majors not requiring advanced math don't lead to specific careers. What, for example, can you do with a major in English? You could go on to graduate school. A few people with *specific career plans* can make good use of the "no" majors. Some people with such majors are lucky and find jobs that interest them; and some corporations *like* to hire graduates with liberal arts backgrounds and then train them in the company's methods. You will usually find, however, that college graduates who are unemployed or in low-paying jobs have degrees that did not prepare them for a specific job.

Did You Know?[11]

With math in her background a young woman graduating from high school can expect to earn $2,000-$4,000 more in her first entry level job. Math is often the key to the non-traditional jobs that pay more and offer more upward mobility.

It is a myth that people good at math can instantly come up with right answers or correct procedures.

The average yearly salary offered to a graduate with a 1983 Bachelor of Science Degree in Petroleum Engineering was $31,044; with a Bachelor of Arts Degree in Humanities, $16,560.

These high-paying jobs require some college math.

Doctors
Nurses
Pharmacists
All science-related jobs
examples:
Engineers
Physicists
Geologists
Oceanographers
Architects
Accountants
Computer Programmers

A study in 1974 found that without 3-1/2 years of high school mathematics, entering students at the University of California at Berkeley found 3/4 of the college majors closed to them.

Math is not a talent, but a series of skills to be learned.

Mary Kay's Story

Mary Kay's friends scoffed at her interest in math and science. They said that you should just go to college to have fun and learn interesting things. Mary Kay thought differently. "I decided I wanted to be able to get a job that I'd like, and that would support me just about anywhere in the country. So I went into pharmacology. It sounds boring to a lot of people, I know, but I love it. I've been working at the hospital for eight years now. I work with doctors and patients, and recently I started lecturing to nursing classes. I make more money than most women do, too. I feel badly that some of my old friends still haven't found jobs they like. One of them, though, finally decided to start all over, and is now in medical school. She's the one who was most against my studying pharmacology. Funny how things work out."

Are You Giving Up a High-Paid Future for a Dead-End Job?

Jennifer's Story

At the age of 35, Jennifer was working at a dead-end job with no benefits and no pension. She had considered going to vocational school to become an electrician, but now she thought she was too old, or it would take too much time, or it wouldn't be worthwhile, anyway. Then one night she dreamed she was an old woman, alone and homeless and hungry. She awoke with renewed motivation to check into her options.

Jennifer found she could be trained as an electrician in two years, and that the average salary for that profession is $35,600 a year. She was currently making about half that amount. If she planned to be in the workforce for about thirty more years, she decided, it would be well worth her time to retrain for the higher-paying position.

An investment of time and energy now can pay big dividends in the future. Are you wondering if it's worthwhile to retrain for a new career? Use the following exercise to help you decide.

Compare your current salary with the salary of a non-traditional career that holds some appeal for you.

$_____ (a) minus $ _____ (b) = $_____ (c)
non-traditional job   your job   difference

How many years til you are 65 years old (or the age you hope to be when you retire)?_____(d)

Multiply the difference in salary (c) by the number of years you have left in the workforce (d).

_____ (c) x _____ (d) = _____ (e) the difference in the amount of money you will make in lifetime earnings.

How many years would you need to spend retraining for this career? _____ (f)

How much is each year of training worth in terms of future earning? = (g)

_____ (e) divided by _____ (f) = _____ (g)

In some cases, staying at a dead-end job is a necessity, at least for the present. But if you can afford to make a change now, can you really afford *not* to?

REFLECTIONS

CHAPTER TEN

Putting It All Together

Career planning

You must do the thing you think
you cannot do.
— Eleanor Roosevelt

If you can do it then why do it?
— Gertrude Stein

There are many ways to approach career planning. You can ask your best friend what she's going to do, and do the same. You can ask your in-laws what they want you to do, and then do the opposite. You can put off making any plans in the hope that you'll never have to support yourself (after all, there are still a few unmarried wealthy men in your community). You can cling to your job fantasies, even if the obstacles are very evident. (Who *says* a jockey can't be 40 years old, 5'8" and weigh 130 pounds?) Or, you can do it the right way.

As you've completed the exercises in this book, you have compiled a self-portrait. You know what kind of life style appeals to you, and how much it might cost to support yourself in that manner. You realize that you may well *have* to maintain it alone. You've thought about your values, your goals and your skills. You've considered the changes you would like to make in your life. Now you need to investigate some of the careers that appeal to you — careers that fit the person you are, the woman you hope to become.

Don't be inhibited about what you've done so far. This book is not "Your Life Plan," carved in stone. It's not something you'll be held to forever and ever. As you change, so may your plans. Change is a normal part of life. But don't change blindly. This chapter will teach you how to investigate the jobs that most appeal to you. The process will work just as well next year and the year after that. In fact, it can help you choose, throughout your life, the best job for a very unique person — you.

My Family / Relationship
Goals

_____

_____

_____

My Skills,
Aptitudes,
& Interests

_____

_____

_____

_____

Who are You, Anyway?

Look over the information you've learned thus far. Fill in the balloons to get a picture of yourself.

Job Characteristics

My Values

_____
_____
_____
_____

My Goals

_____
_____
_____
_____
_____

Now that you've reviewed a few of your own characteristics, let's look at some that are job-related. Four important considerations are listed below, along with some of the choices that go along with them. Choose one or two phrases from each category that best describe what you want in a job or work situation.

Environment

Outdoors
Pleasant indoor environment
Lovely office
Shop/garage/warehouse
Some outdoors/some indoors

Other _____
_____

Compensation

Security
High emotional rewards
Recognition in the community
Excitement/adventure
Weekly paycheck
High pay
Flexible time

Other _____
_____

Responsibility

Own boss
Low stress
Variety
Power
Freedom
Team work
Decision maker
Few decisions made
Support/assist/help

Other _____
_____

Working with:

People
Adults
Children
Senior citizens
Poor
Animals
Machines
Hands
No one else

Other _____
_____

Everyone Can't be a Superstar

Considering all the things you know about yourself, what are two careers you think you might like? Be sure to consider all the alternatives. For example, it's easy to think of well-known glamour jobs, and jobs that have great appeal. You might think it would be fun to be a star like Linda Evans. Unfortunately, those jobs are rare. However, if you look beyond the obvious, there are thousands and thousands of different jobs. For every superstar, there are dozens of people on the sidelines. The others may not get their pictures in the paper all the time, but they do take part in all the excitement, meet important people, travel and make a living at it. Perhaps you've never thought about all the "behind the scenes" jobs. Here are just a few of them, to get you started. Put on your thinking cap and see if you can come up with others and put them on the blank lines. Maybe one of them is *the* job for you.

Behind every television star there's a:

make-up artist	hairdresser	personal secretary
stunt person	photographer	answering service
wardrobe consultant	manager	accountant
agent	writer	caterer
_____	_____	_____
_____	_____	_____

Every brain surgeon needs a:

general physician	dietician	physical therapist
anesthetist	pharmacist	speech pathologist
hospital	secretary	occupational
administrator	x-ray technician	therapist
head nurse		counselor
_____	_____	_____
_____	_____	_____

A movie director can't operate without a:

camera operator	stage hand	props director
light technician	producer	publicity agent
set director	music director	electrician
film editor	cinematographer	special effects designer

_____

_____

Professional athletes use a:

coach	agent	statistician
equipment manager	sportscaster	photographer
doctor	referee/umpire	sportswriter
physical therapist	scoreboard operator	time keeper

_____

_____

If you can't be a rock musician, maybe you can be a:

disc jockey	sound editor	concert co-ordinator
recording technician	record producer	lighting director
piano tuner	song writer	costume desiger
album cover designer	cutting designer	dancer

_____

_____

The President of the United States has at least one:

advisor	chauffeur	Director of Protocol
assistant	pilot	White House tour guide
speech writer	chef	interior designer
security guard	secretary	press secretary

_____

_____

The Chief Executive Officer of a major oil corporation is backed by a:

corporate planner	lobbyist	computer programmer
accountant	geologist	data entry operator
lawyer	petroleum engineer	financial analyst
marketing manager	publicity director	researcher

_____

_____

What would you like to do? List two choices below. They might be in fields you've been thinking about for a long time, or they could be jobs that have occurred to you since you started doing these exercises. You don't have to know a lot about them. That's the purpose of this exercise. *Let your imagination soar here.*

1. _____

2. _____

Choose *one more* job from the following list. These are non-traditional careers that women often overlook even though they can be very rewarding and high-paying.

Carpenter	Plumber
Pilot	Architect
Telephone repairer	Garbage collector
Truck driver	Gardener
Computer programmer	Hotel manager
Doctor	Broadcaster
Auto mechanic	Insurance salesperson
Lawyer	City manager
Marine biologist	Accountant
Mechanical engineer	House painter
Police officer	Geologist
Stockbroker (account executive)	Welder

3. _____

Gathering Job Information

To find out about the jobs you've chosen, you'll need to go to your public library. *The Occupational Outlook Handbook* discussed in the previous chapter will give you much of the information you will need. Another good source is the *Dictionary of Occupational Titles*, or DOT. In addition, ask the librarian to direct you to the section with career materials. Here you'll find many books which may deal in greater depth with jobs you're investigating. For example, there may be recent books on jobs for women, blue collar jobs, technical jobs, sales, and so forth. Become familiar with these sources, because they can provide you with important facts and figures whenever you think of an interesting new job, or later in life, when you think you'd like to change careers.

Once you've selected the three careers you want to look at more closely, answer the following questions about each of them. Separate worksheets are included for each career.

Job title _____

1. List specific activities to be performed on the job. (Some examples would be: "Carpenter — measuring, sawing, hammering, sanding; Lawyer — researching, writing, interviewing clients, giving speeches in courtroom.")

_____
_____
_____

2. What is the job environment? Is the job done indoors or outdoors? In a large office? In a noisy factory?

_____

3. What rewards does the job provide? High salary? Convenient hours? Emotional satisfaction? Pleasant surroundings? Adventure?

_____
_____

4. Why would this job be particularly satisfying to *you*? Review your values, interests, and life goals for guidance here.

_____
_____
_____

5. How much training or education is required? Where could you get it? (Some examples are: a four-year degree from a university, six months at a business or trade school.) If possible, try to find a specific school or place where you could receive the training you would need. Not all colleges offer degrees in architecture, marine biology, and so forth.

_____
_____
_____

6. Are there any physical limitations? If so, what are they? (Strength requirements, health requirements, 20/20 vision, etc.)

_____
_____

7. What is the approximate starting salary for this job? Mid-career salary?

_____
_____
_____

8. What is the projected outlook for this occupation? Will there be many jobs available when you are ready to enter the job market? Or are there few openings with much competition?

_____

_____

_____

_____

9. What aptitudes, strengths and talents are required?

_____

_____

_____

_____

10. How can you begin today to prepare for this career?

_____

_____

_____

_____

11. What classes do you need to take to pursue this career?

_____

_____

_____

_____

12. Where would you find employment in this job in your community or state?

_____

_____

_____

Job title _____

1. List specific activities to be performed on the job. (Some examples would be: "Carpenter — measuring, sawing, hammering, sanding; Lawyer — researching, writing, interviewing clients, giving speeches in courtroom.")

_____

_____

_____

2. What is the job environment? Is the job done indoors or outdoors? In a large office? In a noisy factory?

_____

_____

3. What rewards does the job provide? High salary? Convenient hours? Emotional satisfaction? Pleasant surroundings? Adventure?

_____

_____

_____

4. Why would this job be particularly satisfying to _you_? Review your values, interests, and life goals for guidance here.

_____

_____

_____

_____

5. How much training or education is required? Where could you get it? (Some examples are: a four-year degree from a university, six months at a business or trade school.) If possible, try to find a specific school or place where you could receive the training you would need. Not all colleges offer degrees in architecture, marine biology, and so forth.

_____

_____

_____

_____

6. Are there any physical limitations? If so, what are they? (Strength requirements, health requirements, 20/20 vision, etc.)

_____

_____

_____

7. What is the approximate starting salary for this job? Mid-career salary?

_____

_____

_____

8. What is the projected outlook for this occupation? Will there be many jobs available when you are ready to enter the job market? Or are there few openings with much competition?

_____

_____

_____

_____

9. What aptitudes, strengths and talents are required?

_____

_____

_____

10. How can you begin today to prepare for this career?

_____

_____

_____

11. What classes do you need to take in high school to pursue this career?

_____

_____

_____

12. Where would you find employment in this job in your community or state?

_____

_____

_____

Job title _____

1. List specific activities to be performed on the job. (Some examples would be: "Carpenter — measuring, sawing, hammering, sanding; Lawyer — researching, writing, interviewing clients, giving speeches in courtroom.")

_____

_____

_____

_____

2. What is the job environment? Is the job done indoors or outdoors? In a large office? In a noisy factory?

_____

_____

3. What rewards does the job provide? High salary? Convenient hours? Emotional satisfaction? Pleasant surroundings? Adventure?

_____

_____

_____

4. Why would this job be particularly satisfying to *you*? Review your values, interests, and life goals for guidance here.

_____

_____

_____

_____

5. How much training or education is required? Where could you get it? (Some examples are: a four-year degree from a university, six months at a business or trade school.) If possible, try to find a specific school or place where you could receive the training you would need. Not all colleges offer degrees in architecture, marine biology, and so forth.

_____

_____

_____

_____

6. Are there any physical limitations? If so, what are they? (Strength requirements, health requirements, 20/20 vision, etc.)

_____

_____

_____

7. What is the approximate starting salary for this job? Mid-career salary?

_____

_____

_____

8. What is the projected outlook for this occupation? Will there be many jobs available when you are ready to enter the job market? Or are there few openings with much competition?

_____

_____

_____

_____

9. What aptitudes, strengths and talents are required?

_____

_____

_____

_____

10. How can you begin today to prepare for this career?

_____

_____

_____

_____

11. What classes do you need to take to pursue this career?

_____

_____

_____

12. Where would you find employment in this job in your community or state?

_____

_____

_____

Ask an Expert

Another valuable way to learn *a lot* about careers is to interview someone who already does the work you're considering. Just calling someone you may not even know, and asking her or him to spend some time with you, may sound frightening, but don't worry. This technique, called the informational interview, is highly recommended by many employment counselors and career experts. Most people love to talk about themselves, and will be happy to give you an appointment. Just remember that this person is probably making room for you in a tight schedule, so be on time, be polite, and don't stay longer than you said you would. Afterwards, send a thank you note. Use this technique to interview someone currently working in each of the occupations that interests you.

If you don't know the name of someone working in the field you wish to investigate, ask your friends, relatives or instructors. Consult a phone book, a librarian, the Chamber of Commerce, professional organizations, unions, an agricultural extension agent, an employment office, or another source which might deal with people in that profession.

Once you have a name and phone number, you're set to make a call. You might start the conversation by saying something like this: "Hello, Ms. Jones. This is Steve Smith. I'm interested in becoming an accountant and my friend, Betty Johnson, suggested I talk with you to get a better idea of what it's like. Would you be able to spare half an hour to answer some of my questions?"

The questionnaire provided here will help you guide the interview.

INTERVIEW QUESTIONNAIRE

Job title _____

Male or female? (You shouldn't need to ask this one!) _____

How many years have you been in this job? _____

_____

What is your personal educational history? _____

_____

_____

_____

If you had your educational years to live over again, what would you do differently?

_____

_____

What advice would you give me as I begin my career search and preparation?

_____

_____

What do you like best about your job?

_____

_____

What do you like least about your job?

_____

_____

Do you foresee a career change before you retire?

_____

_____

If so, to what type of work? _____

_____

_____

Getting Experience

Once you think you've made a decision and know which career you want to pursue, there's a valuable step you can take. It will either reinforce your decision, or help you change your mind before you've invested a great deal of time and money. It's this: Get experience in your chosen field. Of course, an inexperienced person can't go out and get a job as a surgeon or an architect. However, you can usually find something to do that will put you in contact with the job and the people who do it. You may have to take a part-time job at the minimum wage to run errands in an engineering office or at a construction site, or wherever your prospective job is performed. Would you like to be a chef? A waitressing job or one as a preparations assistant in the kitchen would help you decide. What would it be like to be a trial lawyer? Attend a court trial to learn. What does an urban planner do? You could see one in action by attending a city planning commission meeting. Interested in communications? Visit a TV or radio station and find out what the people you see and hear do when they're not in front of a camera or microphone. Even if you have to *volunteer* your time, you'll find it worthwhile. In fact, doing volunteer work is a valuable way not only to gain experience, but to learn new skills and meet people who might be able to help you in your career, as well.

Pat's Story

Pat, for example, wanted to be a lawyer. She passed up a higher-paying job to be a receptionist at a local law firm. She learned what goes on in a law firm. That made her more determined than ever to go through with her law school plans. Just being in the environment also helped her pick up a lot of information which made her school work easier. She could see why different classes were important, and was less tempted to let her work slip. All this time the lawyers in the office encouraged her and observed her progress. When she graduated from law school, they offered her a job. Today she is partner in the firm.

Mindy's Story

Mindy, on the other hand, had been sure since the second grade that she wanted to be a veterinarian. She loved animals, and the course work was easy enough. The summer after her junior year of college, she took a job at a veterinary clinic. She hated it. She didn't like the hours. She realized that this would stand in the way of a family life. She found the tasks boring and repetitive, because only a small percentage of the time was spent in surgery. Though it was difficult for her to give up her dream, she decided that she needed a more creative job with more freedom and more varied duties. Fortunately, she changed her plans before spending four years in veterinary school. Of course, she didn't give up her passion for animals— she now breeds thoroughbred horses as a sideline.

What about you? How can you get first-hand experience in your chosen career? Whatever you have to do, or whatever else you have to give up, it will be one of the most valuable experiences you can have!

Your Goals

By now you should have some ideas about what you want for your future, in terms of both your career and your family. What are your goals for the future?

ONE YEAR FROM NOW

Goal _____

Objectives _____

_____

_____

Goal _____

Objectives _____

_____

_____

AFTER COMPLETING MY TRAINING

Goal _____

Objectives _____

_____

_____

Goal _____

Objectives _____

_____

_____

REFLECTIONS

CHAPTER ELEVEN

Yes You Can!

Financial aid for school or training

If there's a will, there's a way.

Where do you go from here? Chances are, you'll need some type of training. That might mean college, junior college, vocational or business school or an apprenticeship. Whatever you choose, it will probably require money, and that's why a lot of people get discouraged. Don't let yourself be one of them.

Financial aid is available to almost everyone — *if* you know where to look, and, if you keep these two rules in mind:

1. Apply for every type of aid for which you are qualified.
2. Apply on time.

It is never too soon to start your search for financial aid. Where should you look? Information is readily available. Look in libraries, book stores, and career centers, under the topic of "financial aid" or "student financial aid." A counselor at your community college receives all the latest bulletins, and should have files of local aid sources. The schools you are applying to also have extensive, free financial aid information. You need only write to the school and request it.

What school should you contact? At this point, you probably don't know where you want to go, much less where you'll be accepted. Get all the information you can to assure that you make the best choice. Write for bulletins and financial aid information from many sources: private colleges, state universities, state colleges, junior colleges and vocational-technical schools. The library at a local college has names and addresses for these.

Before choosing schools, you will need to know approximately how much money you will need for the following items.

- Tuition and fees (stated in school catalogue)
- Books and supplies (approximations stated in catalogue)
- Room and board (The cost is stated in catalogue for living on campus. Otherwise, use cost of living at home or in an apartment.)
- Transportation (daily, if commuting from home; two round trips per year, if school is distant)
- Personal expenses (clothing, laundry, recreation, etc.)
- If you have a family to support this must be factored in.

Compare sample budgets for each of the schools you are considering.

ESTIMATED EXPENSES

	Sample Budget	First College Choice	Second College Choice	Third College Choice
Tuition	$3,000	_____	_____	_____
Books and supplies	300	_____	_____	_____
Room and board	1,700	_____	_____	_____
Personal	600	_____	_____	_____
Transportation	400	_____	_____	_____
Other	_____	_____	_____	_____
TOTAL	**$6,000**	_____	_____	_____

ESTIMATED RESOURCES

Less	Sample Budget	First College Choice	Second College Choice	Third College Choice
Income in excess of expenses	$1,000	_____	_____	_____
Summer savings	500	_____	_____	_____
Personal savings	300	_____	_____	_____
Other	_____	_____	_____	_____
TOTAL	**$1,800**	_____	_____	_____
Equals **ADDITIONAL FUNDS NEEDED**	$4,200	_____	_____	_____

For most types of aid, you and your family are expected to contribute as much as you are able. This amount is determined by completing an application which takes into account the size and income of your family. By subtracting the expected family contribution from the total estimate for your year's expenses, you will come up with the amount of financial aid you need. Until the standardized needs assessment is completed, you will not know exactly what you or your family are expected to contribute. *Do not wait to find* this figure before applying. It will be too late. Remember that you are under no obligation to accept anything until you formally enroll in the school. *Then* you can determine if the package and the program meet your needs.

To maximize your chances for a favorable package, you should normally apply for financial aid at the same time you apply for enrollment. It is highly recommended that you contact the financial aid officer at your chosen school nine months to a year before you plan to enroll.

Ninety percent of all financial aid is channeled through financial aid officers at post high school educational facilities. We repeat: You should learn what's available, and apply to the appropriate sources on time. It will, literally, pay off.

What is Available?

Financial aid is of three types:

- Gift aid
- Loans
- Work study

GIFT AID: SCHOLARSHIPS AND GRANTS

Scholarships and grants are paid to the student or the school and do not have to be repaid. Sometimes they are based on financial need, but in other cases, they are awarded on the basis of academic achievement or some other specific criteria, such as participation in athletics, excellence in music, art, or writing. There are also a large number of restricted grants or scholarships. Qualifying for these depends on having a particular ethnic background, or religious affiliation, or on studying in a certain field.

Be sure to search widely. There are literally thousands of grants and scholarships available.

LOANS

Loans, unlike gift aid, must be paid back, usually with interest. The interest rate is usually much lower than the commercial interest rate, and the terms allow recipients to pay back their loans after they finish school.

WORK-STUDY

Additional sources of financing can be obtained from student employment or work-study programs. Often the jobs available are related to your chosen field of study and can provide valuable experience. Work-study jobs are also flexible enough to meet the time commitments of students.

In addition, you may be eligible for other specific benefits. Support from railroad or veteran's benefits, are available to many families. The military also offers its own plans for education and training.

ANOTHER OPTION: WORKING YOUR WAY THROUGH

You might consider the possibility of working your way through college or trade school. It's not easy, and it may take you a little longer to graduate, but it can be done in a number of ways.

If you can live at home, or if you have saved some money, you may be able to make ends meet just by working part-time during the school year and full-time over the summer. If you need a full-time income, you may have to take fewer classes each term. In many schools, degrees in some subjects can be earned entirely through evening classes. Or, you might want to work full-time, save your money, and postpone your education for a year or two.

If your efforts don't initially produce a source of financial aid, keep looking. You've come too far to turn back now.

The adventure's just beginning.

REFLECTIONS

Time is a dressmaker specializing
in alterations.
— Faith Baldwin

CHAPTER TWELVE

What Are You
Doing For the
Rest of Your Life?

Exercises for the future

We should all be concerned about
the future because we will have to
spend the rest of our lives there.
— Charles F. Kettering

Way back in the beginning of this book, we promised that this would be your story. If we've been at all successful, you realize by now that what happens to you from here onward is pretty much up to you. You are the author of your own life story.

In these pages, you can record the changes that will take place in the coming years. You can expect substantial changes in your goals and values. And, whatever your age, there will always be new decisions to be made. The skills you have acquired while working through this journal will prove useful throughout your life. When your world seems particularly puzzling, you may want to refer back to the appropriate chapter and review how to make a decision, or how to figure out what it is that you want.

Use the following pages to help you remember where you've been, and where you're heading. Someday you might want to pass your book on to a granddaughter or other young woman. We hope that the message you'll give to her will be full of hope, fulfillment, and resounding success!

Five Years From Now

Age _____   Photo

Date _____

Thoughts about relationships:

Experiences I've found most valuable or satisfying:

What I value now:

My family plans and goals:

Important decisions I must make:

How I spend my time:

New skills and interests:

My goals for the next ten years:

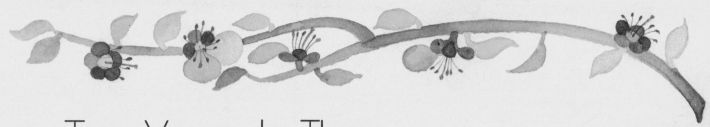

Ten Years In The Future

Age _____   Photo

Date _____

Values I'd like to instill in my children:

Experiences I've found most valuable or satisfying:

What I value now:

My family plans and goals:

Important decisions I must make:

How I spend my time:

New skills and interests:

My goals for the next ten years:

15 Years In The Future

Age _____   Photo

Date _____

Mid-life changes I'm considering:

Experiences I've found most valuable or satisfying:

What I value now:

My family plans and goals:

Important decisions I must make:

How I spend my time:

New skills and interests:

My goals for the next ten years:

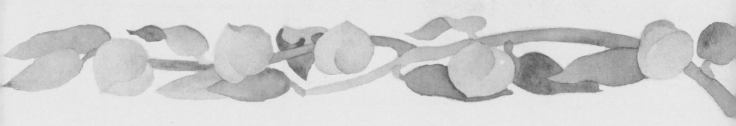

20 Years In The Future

Age _____   Photo

Date _____

How I feel about getting older:

Experiences I've found most valuable or satisfying:

What I value now:

My family plans and goals:

Important decisions I must make:

How I spend my time:

New skills and interests:

My goals for the next ten years:

My Retirement Years

Age _____   Photo

Date _____

How I feel about retirement:

Experiences I've found most valuable or satisfying:

What I value now:

My family plans and goals:

Important decisions I must make:

How I spend my time:

New skills and interests:

My goals for the retirement years:

Some Special
Situations

In living your life, you will encounter some special situations. These are the "biggies," the turning points in your life and the decisions that can have a lasting effect on you and on others. You won't come across all of the situations — you may have already encountered some — but more are sure to occur in the future.

The exercises that follow will be helpful when you find yourself confused, lost, or just overwhelmed. Look through them briefly now, and make a mental note that they're here to help you when, and if, the time comes.

Choosing My Partnerships

Choosing a husband, deciding whether to stay married, and choosing a business partner are some of the most important decisions you will make. What's best for you? The following exercise will help you decide.

The first question to ask yourself is, "Is this the right time for me to enter this partnership?" Also, ask yourself, "Am I both emotionally and financially ready for this commitment?"

Use the decision-making process discussed earlier, on page 133, to work through this question.

1. Your goal _____

_____

Alternative	Advantages	Disadvantages	Probable Outcome

What About Your Values?

Partners who share similar values are more likely to have successful marriages or business relationships. Do you share the same values? Have you re-examined *your* values recently? If not, this is the time to do it. Go back to pages 93-97 for review. Then, when you've completed this exercise, ask your partner to fill it out too. Compare your answers.

Your values   Date _____   Your partner's values   Date _____

_____   _____

_____   _____

_____   _____

Teaming up with someone whose goals coincide with yours also increases your chance for happiness or success. Review the section on goal setting starting on page 106. Then, sit down with your partner and write some goals and objectives as they relate to:

Your Relationship

Goal _____

Objectives _____

_____

Your Environment/Locale/Housing

Goal _____

Objectives _____

_____

Career/Work/Economics

Goal _____

Objectives _____

_____

Family/Children/Childcare/Mixing Career and Family

Goal _____

Objectives _____

_____

If you are considering marriage, what are your values concerning children?

	You	Your Fiancé
To have?	_____	_____
When?	_____	_____
How many?	_____	_____
Childcare?	_____	_____

Now That I'm a Mother

With motherhood comes a whole new set of questions: How can one chocolate cookie stretch far enough to cover three chairs, two walls, and an entire two-year-old child? If your maternity ward roommate left the hospital in a pair of size 8 jeans, why are you, six months later, still in maternity pants? Is there a physiological reason why men do not hear the cries of their children during Monday night football or anytime between the hours of midnight and seven a.m.? With all these weighty matters on your mind, you probably haven't had time to think about the kinds of values you hope to instill in your child.

But it's a fact that many values are formed during the pre-school and early school years. Review the values section of this book, pages 87 to 102. From the list provided there, choose the ones you think you would like your children to grow up with. List them here.

_____

_____

_____

_____

Now think of ways you can expose your children to an appreciation for these values, starting now. Write some goals and objectives below. For example, if your goal is to raise independent children, your objectives might include making sure that they are responsible for certain household chores, or restraining yourself from doing things for your children that they are capable of doing for themselves.

Goal _____

Objectives _____

_____

Goal _____

Objectives _____

_____

Goal _____

Objectives _____

_____

Messages I'd Like to Give My Daughter

Back on page 18, you completed an exercise which asked you to consider what messages you would give your daughter on the importance of success in school, appearance, marriage, career, and children. Now that you actually do have a daughter, review that exercise. Have your ideas changed? The passage of time and the realities of adult life make it highly likely. We've reprinted the entire exercise here to let you either re-affirm or re-evaluate your plan. Only this time, we're asking you to think about ways in which you can deliver the messages, as well. Write your messages and action plans below. Even if your daughter is 33 years old, won't it be nice to go to lunch and discuss what *you've* learned?

Success in School: _____

Action Plan: _____

Appearance: _____

Action Plan: _____

Marriage: _____

Action Plan: _____

Career: _____

Action Plan: _____

Children: _____

Action Plan: _____

Let's not leave out the boys. If we hope to achieve an improved life for women, we'll need the help of the other half of humanity. What messages would you like to give your son, and how might you get those messages across to him? Complete the exercise again with your male child in mind.

Success in School: _____

Action Plan: _____

Appearance: _____

Action Plan: _____

Marriage: _____

Action Plan: _____

Career: _____

Action Plan: _____

Children: _____

Action Plan: _____

Help for the Overwhelmed

Looking back, when you were young and someone asked you what you were going to be when you grew up, would the most truthful answer have been "tired"? If so, this exercise may help you get a grip on things. Use it when it all gets to be too much — when you're trying to balance family responsibilities, a career, a relationship, civic activities, possibly a family crisis, and you just can't seem to say "no" to even the most unreasonable requests.

Review the material concerning time management on page 168-171. Then, in the space provided here, list all the tasks you have to do in the next week. Place an A, B, or C next to each to indicate its importance. Next to each C, write an assertive response to use when informing someone of your inability to complete the task.

Continue this practice each week until you gain better control of your time and well-being.

_____ _____

_____ _____

_____ _____

_____ _____

_____ _____

_____ _____

_____ _____

_____ _____

_____ _____

An Exercise for Everyone

PLANNING FOR THE UNFORESEEN

No matter how well you've planned, or how well things seem to be going, circumstances can change drastically overnight. Review the stories on pages 49 to 54 for a small sample of what can go wrong. If you suddenly found you needed to support yourself, could you do it? It's dangerous not to have an alternate plan. Therefore, every woman should do this economic inventory to see where she stands. The tenth anniversary of owning this book might be a good time to check out your capacity for survival.

My income per month, or what I could reasonably expect to earn if I got a job tomorrow: $_____.

Monthly expenses today:

Housing	$ _____
Transportation	$ _____
Clothing	$ _____
Food	$ _____
Entertainment	$ _____
Furnishings	$ _____
Health care	$ _____
Child care	$ _____
Savings	$ _____
Miscellaneous	$ _____
TOTAL	$ _____

If your monthly budget totals more than you now make, or could expect to earn, revise the figures until you've arrived at a budget you could meet.

Housing	$ _____
Transportation	$ _____
Clothing	$ _____
Food	$ _____
Entertainment	$ _____
Furnishings	$ _____
Health care	$ _____
Child care	$ _____
Savings	$ _____
Miscellaneous	$ _____
TOTAL	$ _____

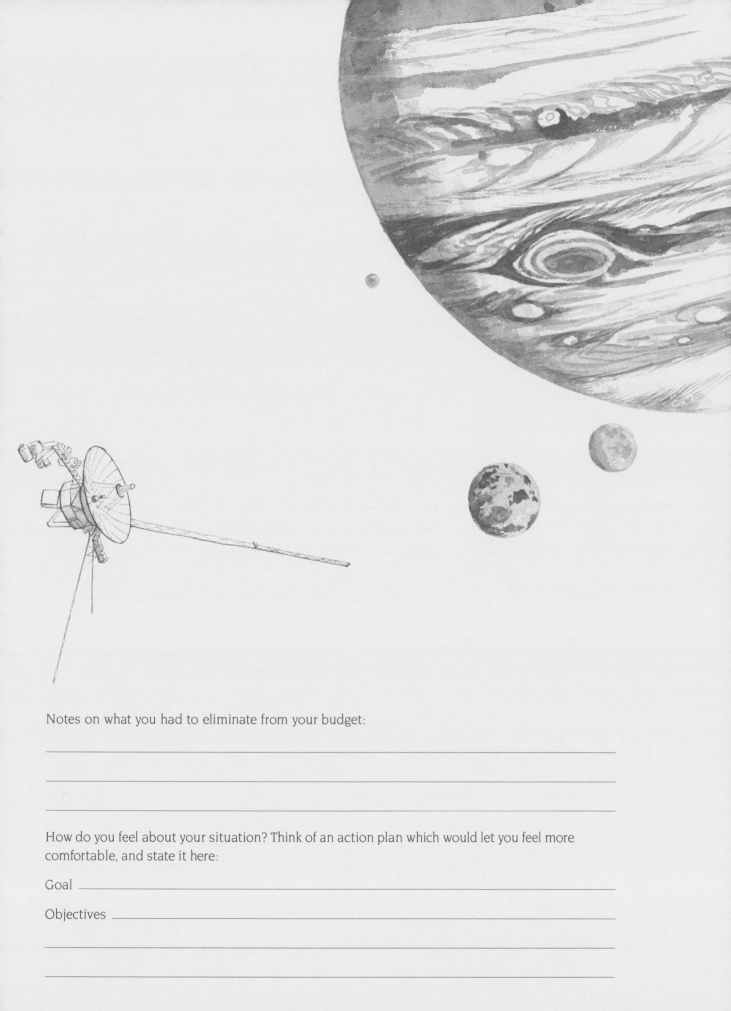

Notes on what you had to eliminate from your budget:

_____

_____

_____

How do you feel about your situation? Think of an action plan which would let you feel more comfortable, and state it here:

Goal _____

Objectives _____

_____

_____

Should I Change Careers?

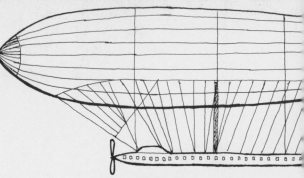

Everyone gets disenchanted with her job from time to time. If that's your situation right now, the first question to ask yourself is if this is a temporary discouragement, or if you're really ready to make a career change.

There is naturally some risk involved in changing jobs. But, there may be a risk in staying where you are, as well. (If, for example, the job doesn't pay enough for you to live on, if you're nearing the point of career burnout, or if you know that your company is in danger of going out of business.) Review the ideas on pages 137-139 to help evaluate and deal with the risks in your particular situation. Dissatisfaction with your present career may be the result of a change in values. What were your values when you took your present job?

_____

_____

What are they now?

_____

_____

Are there external forces prompting this change? (For example, a need for more money, a need for more time, or a desire to relocate.)

_____

_____

Are the risks involved in making a change worth taking? Use the process outlined on page 139 to help you make your decision.

Goal: _____

Alternative	Advantages	Disadvantages	Probable Outcome

If you made a decision, think of an action plan to help you reach your goal.

Goal: _____

Objectives: _____

_____

I've Decided to Change Careers

You've decided to make a career change. Whether you're seeking a job that offers more pay, more potential, more commitment, less time, or less frustration, this career research exercise will help you choose wisely and put your plan into action. Ask yourself the following questions about your new direction and the career you think you want.

Job title _____

1. List specific activities to be performed on the job.

_____

_____

_____

2. What is the job environment? Is the job done indoors or outdoors? In a large office? In a noisy factory?

_____

_____

_____

3. What rewards does the job provide? High salary? Convenient hours? Emotional satisfaction? Pleasant surroundings? Adventure?

_____

_____

_____

4. Why would this job be particularly satisfying to *you*? Review your values, interests, and life goals for guidance here.

_____

_____

_____

5. How much training or education is required? Where could you get it?

_____

_____

_____

6. Are there any physical limitations? If so, what are they? (Strength requirements, health requirements, 20/20 vision, etc.)

_____

_____

_____

7. What is the approximate starting salary for this job? Mid-career salary?

_____

_____

_____

8. What is the projected outlook for this occupation? Are there many jobs available, or are there few openings and much competition?

_____

_____

_____

9. What aptitudes, strengths and talents are required?

_____

_____

_____

10. How can you begin today to prepare for this career?

_____

_____

_____

11. What classes do you need to take to pursue this career?

_____

_____

_____

12. Where would you find employment in this job in your locale?

_____

_____

_____

13. How will this change affect your family?

_____

_____

_____

Filling the Gaps

When your life is running over with family and career obligations, you may think that it would be paradise to have all that time to yourself. There are so many things you want to do; so many places you want to go. Then, when you find yourself with time on your hands — whether because the children have left home, you are widowed or divorced, or you've reached that longed-for retirement — you don't know what to do with it. Your dreams of the past may seem silly or extravagant, or maybe you've bought into the myth that you're too old to try anything new. Of course, you're not! You've earned this time, so go ahead and make it the rewarding part of your life it's meant to be! The exercise below will help you recapture some of those old dreams, and put you on your way to making them come true.

My hobbies and avocations are:

_____

_____

_____

I keep current and active in these areas by:

_____

_____

_____

If I had three wishes, they would be:

1. _____

2. _____

3. _____

What I can do, starting now, to make sure my wishes become a reality.

Goal _____

Objectives _____

_____

Goal _____

Objectives _____

_____

Goal _____

Objectives _____

_____

My Retirement

Retirement can be a shock to your system. You're used to being active; your days have been structured with work you valued and were rewarded for. It's not uncommon for a retired person to feel bored, restless and unneeded. But it's wholly unnecessary to feel that way. You still have the wisdom and the talents you've developed over the years. You only need to find some new outlets for them.

Turn back to the skills identification exercise on page 178. Think of all the skills you've added since then, and write them here.

What an impressive list! Don't let your talents be lost to the world. Think of all the ways you can put this tremendous reservoir of skills to use. Maybe you'd like to start a part-time business or do volunteer work for a social agency. There are hundreds of possibilities. Write down all you can think of here, and put the vitality back into your life!

My Legacy to the World

You've touched thousands of lives during your years on this earth. You've had friends and enemies, successes and failures, satisfaction and regret. Though much will be forgotten, your life will have an impact on those around you. Have you considered what kind of impact you would like that to be?

I would like to be remembered for:

An open letter to my granddaughters, grandnieces, their daughters and the generations that follow me.

Date _____

INDEX

NOTES

1. Twilla C. Liggett, Patricia L.R. Stevens, and Nan S. Schmeling, *The Whole Person Book: Toward Self-Discovery & Life Options*, under a grant from the Women's Educational Equity Act Program, U.S. Department of Education (Newton, MA: Education Development Center, 1979), pp. 175-176.

2. Coon, Dennis. *Introduction to Psychology: Exploration and Application*, 2nd ed. (St. Paul, MN: West Publishing Co., 1980).

3. Inge K. Broverman, Donald M. Broverman, Frank E. Clarkson, Paul S. Rosenkrantz, and Susan R. Vogel. "Sex Role Stereotypes and Clinical Judgements of Mental Health," *Journal of Consulting and Clinical Psychology*: (1970), vol. 34, no. 1, pp. 1-7. Copyright by the American Psychological Association. Adapted by permission of the publisher and authors.

   Also adapted from Liggett, Stevens and Schmeling, *The Whole Person Book: Toward Self-Discovery & Life Options*.

4. See *20 Facts on Women Workers*, U.S. Department of Labor, Office of the Secretary, Women's Bureau (1984) for quiz nos. 2,4,6,7.

   See *Today's Girls — Tomorrow's Women*, (A National Seminar, June 13-15, 1978, Wingspread Conference Center, Racine, Wisconsin, reprint ed., Girls Clubs of America, Inc., 1980) for quiz nos. 1,9,10

   See Liggett, Stevens and Schmeling, *The Whole Person Book: Toward Self-Discovery & Life Options*, for quiz no. 8.

   See Bureau of Labor Statistics, Department of Labor, March 1984, for quiz no. 3.

   See "Factsheet On Women," American Council of Life Insurance, Community and Consumer Relations, Fall 1983, for quiz no. 5.

5. Richard Boyer and David Savageau, *Places Rated Almanac: Your Guide to Finding the Best Places to Live in America* (Rand McNally and Co., 1981).

6. U.S. Department of Agriculture, Human Nutrition Information Service, Consumer Nutrition Center (Hyattsville, Md.).

7. H. B. Gelatt, Barbara Varenhorst, and Richard Carey, *Deciding* (New Jersey: College Board Publications, 1972), p 12.

8. Ibid., p. 44.

9. Earl F. Mellor, "Weekly Earnings in 1983: A Look at More Than 200 Occupations", *Monthly Labor Review*, January 1985, "Research Summaries".

10. Sheila Tobias, "Girls and Mathematics: Overcoming Anxiety and Avoidance," *Voice for Girls* (New York: Girls Clubs of America, Inc., Fall 1982), vol. 26, no. 3.

Manpower Comments, Washington D.C. Scientific Manpower Commission, Vol. 20, No. 4, May 1983.

Manpower Comments, Vol. 20, No. 7, September 1983.

ILLUSTRATIONS

Itoko Maeno, Art Director — Cover, pages 1, 2, 3, 4, 6-7, 8-9, 10-11, 12, 13, 20-21, 24, 25, 26, 27, 28, 29, 30, 31, 32, 33, 34-35, 36, 37, 38, 40-41, 43, 44-45, 49, 50, 51, 52, 53, 54, 55, 56, 59, 60-61, 62-63, 69, 78-79, 82, 86-87, 88, 89, 92, 94, 95, 97, 100, 105, 106, 108, 110, 114-115, 120-121, 122, 123, 124, 128, 132, 134, 135, 136, 138, 140-141, 142, 144, 146, 147, 148, 149, 150-151, 152-153, 154, 155, 162, 165, 166, 167, 168, 170-171, 172-173, 175, 177, 179, 180-181, 186-187, 188, 189, 194-195, 196-197, 198, 200, 201, 202, 204, 206, 208, 209, 231, 232, 235, 237, 238, 240.

Janice Blair — pages 16, 17, 18, 66, 84, 85, 113, 116, 117, 118-119, 125, 126, 127, 130, 131, 137, 182, 184-185, 192.

Pam Hoeft — pages 57, 58, 64-65, 70, 74-75, 77, 80, 91.

Diana Lackner — pages 22, 46, 47, 48, 72, 73, 98, 99, 100, 101, 102, 103, 112, 156, 157, 159, 190-191, 214-215.

Christine Nolt — Production Coordination and pasteup.

Type by Friedrich Typography.

Other books by Advocacy Press:

Choices: A Teen Woman's Journal for Self-awareness and Personal Planning, by Mindy Bingham, Judy Edmondson and Sandy Stryker. Softcover, 240 pages. ISBN 0-911655-22-0. $14.45

Challenges: A Young Man's Journal for Self-awareness and Personal Planning, by Bingham, Edmondson and Stryker. Softcover, 240 pages. ISBN 0-911655-24-7. $14.45

Gifts every parent, grandparent and caring adult will want to give the teenagers in their lives. CHOICES and CHALLENGES engagingly address the myths and hard realities each teenager will face in entering adulthood. They contain thought-provoking exercises that prompt young people to think about their futures, develop quantitative goals, make sound decisions, assert themselves, and evaluate career options, marriage, child-rearing responsibilities and lifestyle budgeting.

Consider using either of these books with your copy of *Changes* for a dynamic mother/daughter or mother/son experience.

More Choices: A Strategic Planning Guide for Mixing Career and Family, by Bingham and Stryker. Softcover, 240 pages. ISBN 0-911655-28-X. $17.45

Traditionally, career planning and planning for a family have been considered separately, as though there is no relationship between these two major spheres of life. MORE CHOICES takes a new approach and shows how, with proper planning, it is possible to support a family—and still find time to enjoy it. This is an ideal book for people about to choose a career, whether they are in high school, college or at re-entry level.

Minou, by Mindy Bingham, illustrated by Itoko Maeno. Hardcover with dust jacket, lovely full-color watercolor illustrations throughout, 64 pages, ISBN 0-911655-36-0. $14.45

This charming children's picture book about a cat in Paris introduces a life concept still, regrettably, missing from much of children's literature—the reality that everyone, especially young women, must be prepared to support themselves. It is everything a children's book should be . . . imaginative, beautiful *and* meaningful.

Father Gander Nursery Rhymes: The Equal Rhymes Amendment, by Father Gander. Hardcover with dust jacket, full color illustrations throughout, 48 pages, ISBN 0-911655-12-3. $14.45

Without losing the charm, whimsy and melody of the original *Mother Goose* rhymes, each of Father Gander's delightful rhymes provides a positive message in which both sexes, all races and ages, and people with a myriad of handicaps interact naturally and successfully.

You can find these books at better bookstores. Or you may order them directly by sending the noted price (includes shipping) to Advocacy Press, P.O. Box 236, Dept. A, Santa Barbara, California 93102. For your review we will be happy to send you more information on these publications.